JAPAN

Dan Colwell

JPMGUIDES

CONTENTS

3	This Way Japan
7	Flashback
17	On the Scene
17	Tokyo and Northern Honshu
35	Kyoto and Kansai Region
53	Western Honshu
61	Hokkaido
69	Shikoku
73	Kyushu
80	Okinawa
82	Cultural Notes
87	Dining Out
93	Shopping
97	Sports
100	The Hard Facts
119	Index

Maps
- 109 Hiroshima
- 110 Hokkaido
- 111 Kyoto
- 112 Kyushu
- 114 Nagasaki
- 115 Okinawa
- 116 Central Tokyo
- 118 Osaka

Fold-out map
Honshu and Shikoku
Greater Tokyo

Nature in all its finery

Extravagant street scene

Traditions and superstitions

Religious ritual

THIS WAY JAPAN

Somehow, Japan manages to be both hyper-modernistic and Western, yet at the same time intensely Eastern and traditional. This remarkable coincidence leads to some strange anomalies, and the balance is sometimes uneasy, but it exerts an irresistible fascination on the inhabitants and visitors alike. You will feel it when you are caught up in the frantic hurly-burly of central Tokyo or standing in the quiet and calm of an ancient temple in Kyoto, swishing past Mt Fuji on a high-speed Bullet Train or dining on *sushi* and *sake* in the gourmet paradise of downtown Osaka.

It is best be seen in the big cities, where you might come across a charming Shinto shrine sheltering beneath an elevated expressway, while tiny, ramshackle shops that seem to have survived from the 19th century rub shoulders with high-rise developments that look as though they've been transported back from the future. You might take part in the age-old, Zen ritual of the tea ceremony in the morning and after lunch pore over cutting edge computers and cameras in shops that are a veritable Aladdin's cave of the latest electrical hardware. Then stroll through a park where a group of besuited salarymen from one of Japan's powerhouse companies are sitting beneath a cherry tree, peering at a particular piece of cherry blossom in celebration of a transitory moment of perfection. For medieval samurai warriors, as for priestly haiku poets and contemporary office workers, the sakura season has always been an occasion that touches the Japanese soul like nothing else on earth.

At the Eastern Edge
The Japanese name for the country is Nihon, popularly translated as the Land of the Rising Sun, a term that originates in the Chinese perspective on it as the country to the east. In many ways it can be seen as the true orient: it is located at the very edge of the great Asian landmass, with little

else beyond it to the east apart from the Pacific Ocean, before the next landfall in California thousands of kilometres away.

The country is made up of four main islands—Honshu, Shikoku, Kyushu and Hokkaido, plus a long string of smaller islands, including Okinawa, to the southwest. It's common to hear Japanese people talk of their country as being small (an idea undoubtedly connected to the fact that 80% of the terrain is mountainous and the majority of the population live in the strip of land along Honshu's southern coast). However, Japan is far bigger than you might at first think. The Japanese archipelago stretches 2,400 km from close to Taiwan in the south right up to Siberia in the north, and with a land area of some 377,835 sq km is larger than Germany.

It's also an active, even volatile landscape, situated at a point where the great tectonic plates of Eurasia and the Pacific crash into each other. This causes up to 1000 tremors each year, and in the past century Japan has suffered two huge earthquakes—in Tokyo in 1923 and Kobe in 1995. The country is dotted with volcanos (Mt Fuji is an extinct conical volcano), and eruptions are relatively common. A positive outcome of all this seismic activity has been the creation of hot springs, found throughout the country and enjoyed by the locals as *onsen*, or hot spring baths.

Protected from wintry Siberian snow by the central chain of mountains and volcanoes, cities such as Tokyo and Osaka offer plenty of opportunities to witness the rising sun all year long. There are cold, sunny winters and hot, semi-tropical summers. Spring and autumn are the best times to be in Japan, when the weather is mild and the blossom and nature spectacular.

A Resilient People

One of the best things about any trip to Japan is the chance to observe the people going about their busy lives. Their society is subtly textured, with hierarchical relationships based on family, work and gender conveyed by a complex range of gestures and linguistic nuance. As such it can be very difficult for outsiders—known, not necessarily pejoratively, as *gaijin*—to get to grips with. But the Japanese are almost always polite towards strangers, and at heart downright friendly.

This friendliness is perhaps based on the security of knowing that the nation has the second-largest economy in the world and is one of the most technologically advanced; or that its 127 million citizens have achieved the world's highest literacy rate and lowest crime rate; or that they share a powerful and remarkably homogenous cultural heritage.

To be sure, they have shown an extraordinary resilience in the face of historical events over the centuries. There are very few places in Japan that haven't been destroyed or damaged due to earthquakes, fires, tsunamis or war, and then rebuilt. The most catastrophic time of all came at the end of World War II, when every major city apart from Kyoto was levelled by aerial bombardment, culminating in the atomic bomb attacks on Hiroshima and Nagasaki. At the time, many commentators believed that Japan would never recover from this, but within a few decades the country had re-emerged as a major player on the world stage.

The effort required to achieve the post-war "economic miracle" demanded considerable sacrifice from the Japanese people, not least in the notoriously diminutive living space available to most families. The excruciatingly long hours expected of the nation's workers led to a Japanese phenomenon first identified in the 1980s: *karoshi*, or death by overwork. Since that time Japan has loosened its stays a little. The country has emerged from recession with a slightly different idea of work-life priorities. The Japanese travel abroad more often. Women have asserted their rights more boldly in relation to family and career, and their expectations have begun to shift accordingly.

Thankfully, friendliness and hospitality towards outsiders remains as dominant a feature of the country as ever. In every shop, bank or noodle bar you go to the staff will cry out *irrashaimase*—"Welcome!" In Japan, you'll discover that the sentiments behind this go beyond formal politeness to the very core of the Japanese character.

The most contemplative Zen garden. The raked sand and 15 carefully placed rocks of the beautiful Zen garden at the **Ryoanji** temple in Kyoto have been inducing philosophical thoughts in visitors since the 15th century.

Rainer Hackenberg

Drum beats announce the beginning and end of ceremonies at the Meiji Shrine.

FLASHBACK

The earliest evidence of human habitation in Japan dates back 30,000 years, though many archaeologists now believe that migration probably came via land bridges with Korea to the west and Siberia to the north at least 200,000 years ago. The early Stone Age peoples of the Palaeolithic Period (30,000– 10,000 BC) were primitive hunter-gatherers who sheltered in caves and pits.

By 10,000 BC, they were able to make pottery. Known as *jomon*, "cord marks", after the patterning used, this is the oldest surviving pottery in the world. The Jomon era gave way to the Yayoi Period in around 400 BC. This more technologically sophisticated culture began in Kyushu and spread rapidly eastwards, and could call on iron and, later, bronze implements. Rice and other crops were produced in greater quantities and the population grew accordingly.

By the 5th or early 6th centuries, the country was under the domination of one kingdom, the Yamato, located in modern-day Nara Prefecture. The current emperor is in a direct line of descent from the Yamato kings, making this the world's longest royal lineage. The Yamato kingdom had in place a hierarchical, status-conscious administrative system and in the mid-6th century adopted and promoted Buddhism as a unifying state religion. Under Shotoku Taishi (574–622) the state's laws were codified, temples were built, and relations with China were strengthened. All that was left was to establish a permanent capital. In 710, the court moved to Nara.

The Nara Period
The establishment of the imperial court at Nara ushered in an era of great cultural richness, centred on Buddhism and driven by the court's desire to learn from the T'ang empire in China. At least four official missions were sent to China during the 8th century, and the grid-pattern layout of Nara was based on the T'ang capital of Ch'ang-an. Under such patrons of learning as the Emperor Shomu, Nara's Buddhist temples—inclu-

ding the magnificent Todaiji—were built, and Chinese scholars were encouraged to move to the city.

However, the imperial connection with Buddhist temples meant that the priests were soon perceived as gaining too much political influence over the emperor. After Shomu's death in 749, the aristocracy fought to reclaim power. The leaders of this movement were the Fujiwara family, who were in effect to become the real power behind the throne for another four centuries. They supported the claim of an emperor who was more sceptical of the priests, and in 794, under Emperor Kammu, they achieved a complete break with the Nara temples by shifting the capital once again.

Rise and Fall of the Heian Era

The new capital was at Heian—modern-day Kyoto—built, like Nara, in the T'ang-style grid pattern. While Kammu was careful to forbid religious interference in affairs of state, he and his successors nonetheless supported Buddhist learning and culture. Over the next 150 years the imperial court reached its zenith in terms of social and artistic refinement.

However, clouds were gathering on the horizon. In its concerns with art, etiquette and protocol, the court had become increasingly divorced from the realities of life beyond Heian. The emperor had decentralized tax collection in order to simplify—and boost—his revenues; but this had led to the rise of powerful local governors, *daimyo* (often junior members of the Fujiwara clan) with their own armies of samurai. And in the court itself, the Fujiwara had created the roles of *sessho* (regent) and *kampaku* (chief councillor), which were initially meant to assist the 9-year-old Emperor Seiwa, but had become hereditary posts for the Fujiwara themselves.

With the decline in the imperial court's power came a corresponding loss of Chinese cultural influence. Many historians see this period as the time when Japanese cultural identity began to assert itself in earnest. The end of the Heian era was marked by an increasing marginalization of the Emperor in Japan's political life and a series of military clashes between competing regional lords to see who would dominate Japan. The eventual winners were the Minamoto from the eastern Kanto region. Related to the imperial line, they left the emperor in nominal authority in Heian, but from 1185 real power was with the military government, the *bakufu* or shogunate, that they had established in Kamakura.

Medieval Japan

One of the greatest generals of his time, Minamoto Yoritomo was the first of the shoguns (the word is a short form of *seii taishogun*, literally "barbarian-quelling generalissimo"). No revolutionary, Yorimoto left most of the levers of state intact, though he was careful to place his own loyalists as military governors in the provinces and to make sure tax revenues came to him. The title of shogun passed onto his sons, but without their father's strength of character they were easily controlled by their mother's family, the Hojo, who took over the shogunate within three generations.

The political situation within Japan was always volatile, but in the 13th century the country faced a far greater threat from overseas. Under the aggressive expansionism of Genghis Khan, the Mongols had conquered Asia as far as the Korean peninsula. In 1274, his grandson, Kublai Khan, launched an invasion force of some 40,000 troops that landed in Kyushu. The shogunate's military vassals there put up stout resistance. Mongol reinforcements

The Five-Storey Pagoda of the Buddhist Kofukuji at Nara was first built in 725. An avenue of red *torii* winds up to the Fushimi Inari Taisha at Kyoto, one of Japan's oldest Shinto shrines.

were sent but, miraculously, were destroyed by a typhoon. Seven years later, the Mongols landed in Kyushu, only to be devastated yet again by a typhoon. The Japanese called these typhoons "divine winds"—*kamikaze*—and some have argued that it led to a long-term idea that the nation was under divine protection. More immediately, though, the cost of fighting the Mongols had put the shogunate and its allies under extreme financial pressure.

Encouraged by this apparent weakness, Emperor Go-Daigo attempted to restore direct imperial rule in Kyoto. With the assistance of disaffected members of the Minamoto family, Ashikaga Takauji and Nitta Yoshisada, the shogunate's base in Kamakura was destroyed in 1333. Given the turbulence of the period, it was almost inevitable that this new alliance wouldn't last long; Takauji turned on Go-Daigo in 1336 and drove him out of Kyoto, setting up a more pliable candidate for emperor on the throne, and establishing his own shogunate in the Muromachi district of the city.

The Muromachi Shogunate saw trade links with China reopen and was characterized by the development of some of Japan's most distinctive cultural institutions—the tea ceremony, ikebana (flower arranging), the Zen garden and the wider enjoyment of No drama. This level of cultural achievement is all the more curious as this period was also one of almost continuous factionalism between rival claimants for the shogunate, and civil war between provincial lords who were now beyond the shogun's control. However, in the late 16th century, three of Japan's most remarkable leaders appeared on the scene and, by a combination of political acumen and military force, brought a political order and cohesion to the nation that would last for more than 250 years.

The Closed Country

The reunification—or, more accurately, the pacification—of the country began under Oda Nobunaga, a provincial lord, or *daimyo*, from what is now Aichi Province. He was a brilliant military leader and the first in Japan to understand how to employ firearms effectively when, at the 1575 Battle of Nagashino, he used 3000 musketeers to devastating effect against a rival lord.

In 1582 Nobunaga died in a military campaign in western Japan, but his retainer, Toyotomi Hideyoshi, carried on the work of unification. Hideyoshi was of peasant origin, but his military talent had been recognized by Nobunaga, and he had risen to become the greatest power in the land. By 1590 he had brought the area from Kyushu to northeast Honshu under his control. He also began the persecution of Christians. Since the first Europeans had arrived in Japan in 1543, more than 150,000 Japanese had been converted to Christianity. Perhaps suspicious that this was European colonization by the back door, he had 26 European and Japanese martyrs crucified in Nagasaki in 1597.

After Hideyoshi's death in 1598 there was a short struggle for power between his son, Hideyori, and his most senior vassal, Tokugawa Ieyasu. The matter was resolved at the 1600 Battle of Sekigahara, near Nagoya, where Iesayu won a decisive victory. Three years later, he formally established the Tokugawa Shogunate, which had its power base at Edo (now Tokyo) and kept a firm grip on the nation for the following two centuries. This was achieved by a variety of means beyond military power. There were strict regulations for military families: any sign of insubordination was met with ruthless punishment; social mobility between classes was forbidden; no one was allowed to travel within the country without officially approved documents, and secret police spied on the population.

On top of this, the country was closed to foreigners. The Portuguese were forbidden to enter

Rainer Hackenberg

Tea time. Attending a tea ceremony in an authentic teahouse is one of the essential experiences of any trip to Japan, though it has a lot more to do with ceremony than with drinking tea. The rules were formalized in the 16th century by the Zen teacher, Sen no Rikyu (1522–91), and it became popular with great samurai warriors such as Toyotomi Hideyoshi. Ritual is strictly observed: each movement of the host—spooning the power into the pot, whisking it up into a thick, green froth, pouring it into the guest's cup—is an expression of order and harmony. The tea itself, which should be drunk in one go, is bitter and not to everyone's taste, though that's not the point. Afterwards, guests examine the exquisitely polished utensils, express their admiration, and leave the teahouse having had a glimpse into a world where beauty and simplicity reign supreme.

Japanese waters, and the Dutch trading post in Nagasaki was the only authorized contact with Europeans until the mid-19th century. This period of hot-house seclusion from the world fostered a new period of cultural attainment, with the development of *bunraku* puppet theatre, *kabuki*, and the *ukiyo-e* artists of Edo. But by the 19th century the political system had begun to stagnate, and when it was finally confronted with the modern firepower at the disposal of a Western nation, it soon crumbled.

The Meiji Restoration

For decades, countries such as Britain and the United States had been clamouring for the Tokugawa government to open up Japan to foreign commerce, but they met with little success. The situation changed in July, 1853, when four American warships under Commodore Matthew Perry sailed into Tokyo Bay and forced the signing of trade agreements. The role of the shogun as "chief barbarian queller" was deeply undermined: 15 years later the Tokugawa regime collapsed.

The Meiji Restoration, which placed the emperor back at the centre of Japanese political life, was completed by 1868. In that year the teenaged Emperor Meiji moved the capital from Kyoto to Edo, renaming it Tokyo (or "Eastern Capital"), and took over the Tokugawa castle as his palace. Rather than a restoration, it was in many ways a revolution. Backing the emperor were reformists who saw a radical programme of westernization as the way forward, and they now set about transforming Japanese society. Under the slogan *fokoku kyohei*, "enrich the country, strengthen the military," Japan underwent rapid industrialization with the express intention of reaching equality with foreign powers; high-level government missions were sent to Europe and America. It also became relatively more democratic, with lands taken from the *daimyo* lords and formed into the prefectures that still exist today. The samurai class and feudal system were abolished and political parties established; in 1889, the first written constitution to appear outside the western world created a bi-cameral Diet (parliament). Hirobumi Ito, one of the key figures behind the Meiji Restoration, became Japan's first prime minister.

After centuries of isolation, Japan's engagement with the outside world had led to an extraordinary change in the country's fortunes, though it meant that southeast Asia now had to deal with a powerful and sometimes belligerent new neighbour. A war with China in 1894–95 saw the

Japanese triumphant, but having to give way—resentfully—under pressure from the European great powers. Ten years later, and backed up by the 1902 alliance with Britain, Japan went to war with Russia. The annihilation of the Russian Baltic fleet in 1905 and the stunning victory that followed enhanced the nation's prestige around the world and, more ominously, strengthened the role of the military in the political arena. In 1910 Korea was annexed. In World War I Japan was on the side of the Allies and largely contented itself with taking over German possessions in China and the Pacific.

After a faltering attempt at greater democracy, the late 1920s saw the rise of the militarists, who believed that overseas military conquest was the answer to the severe economic crisis that occurred during the Great Depression. They seized their chance in 1931, when Japanese troops occupied the whole of Manchuria after claiming that Chinese soldiers had attacked a Japanese train. This was carried out without the approval of the Tokyo government, and it proved powerless to stop the army, giving the militarists even more political influence. Japan withdrew from the League of Nations in 1933 and in 1936 signed the Anti-Comintern pact with Germany. A year later it commenced full-scale military action in China, leading to the infamous massacre of 300,000 civilians in Nanking (Nanjing). Japan was set inexorably along the path to war.

Descent into Catastrophe

Throughout the 1930s, extreme nationalists had been advising that Japan conquer Asia in order to obtain resources for a final showdown with the USA. America had closed its borders to Japanese immigration and been instrumental in trying to prevent Japan's naval build-up. When Japan invaded the French colony of Indochina in 1940 the US froze all Japanese assets and embargoed oil exports. With the accession to power in Tokyo of General Tojo Hideki in October 1941, the militarists were now fully in control, and plans were drawn up for a "pre-emptive" strike on the US fleet stationed at Pearl Harbour in Hawaii. On December 1, Emperor Hirohito (enthroned 1926) gave the formal approval for war, and the attack took place six days later. America immediately declared war on Japan.

At first, Japan's success in the war was extraordinary. The US had retreated; the British were quickly defeated in Malaya and Singapore. Western claims to military supremacy looked weak, and the Japanese were initially

able to present themselves as anti-colonial liberators. They soon proved to be far harsher rulers than the Europeans, but their triumph was to be short-lived. After the destruction of the Japanese fleet at the Battle of Midway in June 1942 and the failure to win the battle for Guadalcanal Island in February 1943, the end was already in sight. In July 1944, the American victory at Saipan brought the Japanese mainland in range of US bombers. Almost every major Japanese city was destroyed over the next year, with the great fire-bombing raid over Tokyo on March 10, 1945 killing around 100,000 people. Still, the Japanese government refused to give an unconditional surrender. With the ferocious fighting for Okinawa in April fresh in their minds, and the fear of an assault on the mainland proper, the Americans detonated atomic bombs over Hiroshima and Nagasaki in August 1945. The shock of America's new weapon was immense and the death toll uncountable, many victims dying months or even years later as a result of radiation exposure. Japan ended the war in total and abject defeat.

From the end of World War II to the early 1970s, Japan's economy soared to unprecedented heights.

Modern Japan

The American occupation of Japan was the first time in its history that the country had been conquered by a foreign power. Several of Japan's war leaders, including General Tojo, were hanged for war crimes, though the American commander Douglas MacArthur found it useful to allow the emperor to remain as the nation's figurehead. However, all claims to divine imperial authority were finally renounced. A new constitution was drawn up containing a "no war" clause—and even today the Japanese technically have no army, merely an extremely well-equipped "Self-Defence Force".

Since the end of World War II Japan has risen dramatically from the ashes. American occupation officially ended in 1952, from which point the country enjoyed unprecedented economic growth until the oil crisis in the early 1970s. Throughout this period, Japan remained a staunch ally of the US in the Cold War with the Soviet Union.

The economy picked up again in the 1980s, leading to the so-called "bubble economy", where easy credit was obtainable based on over-inflated land prices. The bubble burst in 1990–91 and triggered off a major recession from which the country is only just recovering.

Several other difficulties have emerged since the beginning of the third millennium. Japan's support for America in the Iraq War created serious domestic political tensions, while China's rise as a regional superpower and the question of North Korea's nuclear programme loom large. Overall, relations with its Asian neighbours continue to be marred by unresolved political issues dating back to the war years. China accuses Japan of not having faced up to the reality of its military aggression: during a visit to China in 1995, Emperor Akihito (acceded in 1989) expressed his "regrets", but this was seen to fall short of a full apology. The prime minister's 2005 visit to the Yasukuni Shrine in Tokyo, which commemorates Japan's war dead including those executed as war criminals, inspired rioting in Beijing and Seoul.

For all this, Japan remains the world's second-largest economy. It's a leader in manufacturing and the development of cutting edge technologies, and is also the world's largest donor of development aid to Third World countries. Despite the demons of the past, and without losing sight of its great cultural heritage and traditions, Japan has entered the third millennium as one of the most dynamic and forward-looking nations on earth.

Tokyo by night, without a doubt the "City of Blinding Lights".

ON THE SCENE

Around 30 million people live within 50 km of central Tokyo, and the region seems at times like an endless expanse of high-rises and housing blocks, neon-lit pachinko parlours and urban expressways, stretching out across the Kanto Plain until it merges with other conurbations like Yokohama, Japan's second-biggest city, to the south. But even such an adrenaline-rush, 21st-century megalopolis as this offers ready escapes to a calmer, quieter world, with easy excursions to Mt Fuji, the island-studded bay at Matsushima, the mountain temples at Nikko or the historic oceanside town of Kamakura, where the Japan of a bygone age lives on.

Tokyo and Northern Honshu

Tokyo is the nation's political, economic and entertainment capital. Until the early 17th century it was a small fishing village called Edo, but expansion was rapid after it became the power base of the Tokugawa shogunate in 1603. By the 18th century it was one of the largest cities in the world and the centre of Japan's flourishing cultural life. With the imperial court's move to the former shogun's castle following the Meiji Restoration of 1868, Edo became the national capital and was renamed Tokyo. It suffered a catastrophic earthquake in 1923 and the fire-bombing of World War II, both of which incurred terrible casualties and devastated the city, yet somehow it emerged with its spirit intact.

Today, Tokyo is a vast metropolis of around 12 million people. At first sight, the urban sprawl looks discouragingly monotonous, with few of the ancient architectural delights of other great capitals. But there are many jewels to be found, including some of the world's most spectacular modern buildings. The character of the city, whose different districts are like separate villages each with its own flavour, soon starts to assert itself, from the narrow streets redolent of the Edo era around Asakusa to the upmarket fashion districts of Ginza and Shibuya.

City Centre

Central Tokyo fans out from the vast site of the Imperial Palace. To the south is the Akasaka district (not to be confused with the old Asakusa district near the Sumida River), with its government buildings and five-star hotels, and beyond this the trendy entertainment area of Roppongi. The neon-lit razzmatazz of the Ginza lies to the east of the palace, while the controversial Yasukuni Shrine is immediately to the northwest. If you're feeling energetic it's possible to walk around this whole area in a day, though if this proves too daunting there are numerous subway lines you can travel on.

Imperial Palace

The former Edo Castle was home to the Tokugawa shogunate and, in its day, the biggest fortress in the world. It's now the Imperial Palace, the residence of the Japanese royal family. The palace itself, a fairly modest post-1945 structure, is closed to the public, while most of the palace grounds are only open twice a year (January 2 and December 23, the emperor's birthday). However, the plaza at the main entrance allows a good view of the massive walls and wide, squared-off moat—Edo Castle's original inner moat—with its black swans and over-fed carp. Here, too, in a beautiful setting is the Nijubashi Bridge, one of Tokyo's most famous sights, where every visitor comes to pose for a souvenir photograph.

The palace's East Garden has been accessible to all since 1968. A wonderful breathing space in the heart of the city, its flowers and seasonal blossom offer lunchtime therapy to frazzled office workers from the nearby Marunouchi business district. The chief entrance to the garden is the Otemon, formerly the main gate of Edo Castle. Inside, crowning a low hill, you can see some of the massive stones that formed the foundations of the castle's keep.

Akasaka district

Just south of the palace stand some of the solid official buildings of Tokyo: the Supreme Court, the National Theatre and the National Diet (parliament), an odd neoclassical blockhouse capped by a stepped pyramid. The glass boxes of government ministries cluster near Hibiya Park, Japan's first western-style park, laid out in 1903. Among its 200 species of trees are American dogwood, sent here in exchange for Japanese cherry trees planted in Washington, DC.

Roppongi

Immediately south of Akasaka, Roppongi is Tokyo's top nightlife hotspot, with a plethora of smart bars and restaurants. Its popularity was helped no end by the opening of the luxury Roppongi Hills complex, the brainchild of developer Minoru Mori. It mixes restaurants, shops and offices and has, as its centrepiece, the ultra-modern 53-storey Mori Tower. The 52nd floor has stunning 360° views of central Tokyo and an observation deck. Entrance tickets give access to the Mori Art Museum, which is on the top floor and puts on temporary exhibitions of contemporary art.

The Mori Tower somewhat dwarfs the 1958 Tokyo Tower, to the east. Nonetheless, at 333 m this red-and-white structure is taller than its Paris lookalike, the Eiffel Tower. Among its technical functions, the tower transmits radio and TV signals, monitors traffic, measures smog and detects earthquakes. If you're worried about safety, you'll find a reassuring little Shinto shrine on the main observation deck.

Virtually next door to the tower, Zojoji temple has been the seat of Buddhism's Jodo sect for hundreds of years and served as the family temple of the Tokugawa shoguns. Many of the historic buildings have perished in wars and disasters, but the main

Modern Tokyo: Starck's startling Golden Flame tops Asahi Brewery in Asakusa; pancakes in Harajuku.

gate and other surviving features give an inkling of its former grandeur. Both colourful and poignant are the lines of little statues of Jizo, protector of the souls of stillborn children. Mourning mothers dress the images in baby clothes and give them toy windmills to hold.

North of Roppongi Hills, the glass-fronted National Art Center is Japan's biggest art museum. It holds temporary exhibitions and has a library, cafés and a restaurant supervised by Paul Bocuse.

The people's theatre. Two 17th-century prohibitions imposed by the shoguns gave *kabuki* theatre its special character. First they banned women from the stage, creating the tradition of male actors in female roles. Then they stopped spectators carrying swords, so the samurai, who couldn't be seen without them, boycotted the plays. As a result, *kabuki* became an entertainment for the common people, with melodramatic plots, broad humour and plenty of colour. Performances can go on for four or five hours, and nowadays tickets are costly. Recognizing that foreigners won't want to pay that much for an incomprehensible show, no matter how spectacular it may be, the Kabukiza theatre in the Ginza sells lower-priced tickets for short sessions, and rents earphones that provide explanations.

Ginza

Of all the Tokyo shopping and entertainment districts, Ginza is the one whose name has spread around the world. Here, a ten-minute walk east of the Imperial Palace, are big department stores like Wako and Mitsukoshi with their tasteful window displays, specialist shops, restaurants, beer halls and innumerable nightclubs. Fashionable and expensive, Ginza is great for strolling by day or night; even after the stores have closed, brilliant illuminations keep the district aglow.

The Kabukiza Theatre is a Ginza landmark, with its hanging lanterns and medieval-style architecture (the building is actually quite new).

On Chuo-ku, in the heart of Ginza, look out for the Sony Building, which has free, hands-on displays of all the latest electronic equipment, virtual-reality games, and other high-tech gadgetry.

Kitanomaru Park

Retracing your steps back to the Imperial Palace, follow the moat round to the northwest side, to this attractive park containing a number of museums. They include the Science Museum, with interactive displays sure to keep the kids happy, and the National Museum of Modern Art, which has a good collection of Japanese art from the Meiji Restoration till today. Also in the park is the Nippon Budokan, where concerts and martial art competitions are held.

Yasukuni Shrine
Across Yasukuni-dori from the park, this controversial shrine honours all Japan's war dead since the imperial restoration in 1868. As these deaths mostly occurred in expansionist wars in China, the Pacific and Southeast Asia, references to the "defence" of the empire might seem inappropriate, and prime ministerial visits have drawn immense criticism from those countries once occupied by Japanese troops.

The museum next to the shrine spans the transition from medieval to modern warfare, from samurai armour to tanks and carrier-borne aircraft of World War II such as the Model 52 Zero fighter, along with *kamikaze* suicide weapons and bullet-marked cannons from the Battle of Okinawa.

Asakusa
Northeast of the city centre, Asakusa is a district where you can still get a flavour of old Edo. It has Tokyo's most colourful temple at its heart, while Ueno Park to the west is the city's best-known spot for viewing cherry blossom. Meanwhile, south along the Sumida River is the Ryogoku district, packed with Sumo stables and home to the excellent new Edo-Tokyo Museum.

Asakusa Kannon Temple
More properly known as Sensoji, the Asakusa Kannon Temple is reached by way of the Kaminari-mon (Thunder Gate), a striking red-and-white structure with a gracefully curving tile roof. Beyond the gate, a long, riotously animated avenue, Nakamise-dori, is lined with small shops and stalls selling jewellery, clothing, pastries and souvenirs of every imaginable kind. Note halfway along on the left the Dembo-in, or Abbot's Residence, a wooden structure dating from the 18th century and a rare survivor of the incendiary attacks of 1945.

A second great gate, the Hozo-mon, equipped with an outsize Japanese lantern, leads to the main shrine hall, but first you'll come to a bronze urn where local visitors purify themselves in the smoke of burning incense. The hall contains a tiny image of the Goddess of Mercy, the Kannon, within a gold-plated inner shrine; the actual statue has been hidden from sight for more than 1,300 years.

Kappabashi
A five-minute walk from the Kannon temple, this street is lined

with shops supplying the restaurant trade and hence known as Kitchen Town. You can buy anything from sharp kitchen knives to plastic models of sushi or bowls of ramen.

Ueno Park
A 20-minute walk west of Asakusa, Ueno Park is worth a whole day's outing on its own, and not only for its boating lakes, bird life, zoological gardens, children's playgrounds, historic shrines and, in April, its spectacular array of cherry blossom. The park is also the home of the city's main concert hall and a number of major museums.

The Tokyo National Museum in the northern end of the park is not to be missed, containing the most important collection of Japanese art in the world, along with fine displays of archaeology and other Asian art.

The National Museum of Western Art is strongest on the French Impressionists and post-Impressionists, and has over 50 Rodin bronzes, many of them in its sculpture garden.

The National Science Museum is especially informative about earthquakes and volcanoes, while the charming Shitamachi Museum preserves the tiny shophouses, artefacts and atmosphere of working-class Tokyo of the early-20th-century Taisho Period (Shitamachi being the name of the plebeian quarter that was once located around Ueno and Asakusa).

Ryogoku
Another 20-minute walk, this time to the south just across the Sumida River, brings you to an area dominated by the Kokugikan Stadium, where Tokyo's main Sumo wrestling tournaments are held in January, May and September. At other times you'll need to content yourself with the small Sumo Museum inside the stadium. The streets south of Ryogoku JR Station contain several Sumo stables, where members of the public are permitted to watch the giant wrestlers at their early morning training sessions throughout the year.

Edo-Tokyo Museum
This is without doubt Tokyo's best new museum, as well as being a marvellous example of the city's breathtaking architectural audacity, giving the effect of a spaceship that has landed next to the Sumo Stadium. Inside, you'll find full-scale dioramas allowing you to walk through atmospheric recreations of Edo and Meiji period Tokyo.

Sumida River
The Sumida River, flowing into Tokyo Bay, hardly competes with

the Seine or the Thames, but there's much to see—the varied, low bridges, the barges and fireboats, and along the banks quaint old wooden houses, warehouses, modern apartment blocks and parks. Boats can be picked up from Azuma Bridge just south of Asakusa Kannon.

Shibuya and Shinjuku

Tokyo's "West End" is where the city's young crowd like to hang out, from teenagers dressed to shock in Harajuku, to the coolest 20- and 30-somethings checking out the trendy boutiques of Omote-sando and the bars and clubs of Shinjuku.

Here, too, is Tokyo's most important imperial shrine, a place of calm and restraint in the middle of such heady fashion consciousness.

Shibuya

Fast-paced, neon-lit, and with a feel akin to London's Piccadilly Circus, Shibuya is more a place to soak up the atmosphere than focus on any particular sights. But it does have one notable landmark in front of the railway station that will be immediately detectable due to the number of people having their photos taken in front of it: the Hachiko Statue commemorates an Akita dog who used to accompany his master to

Guy Minder

Something fishy. On the waterfront a kilometre south of Ginza's glitz and glamour is a far earthier shopping experience, and one very close to the hearts of most Tokyoites. Handling a staggering 2,250 tons of marine products each day, the Tsukiji Market caters to the city's huge appetite for fish. It's one of the biggest fish markets in the world, while the range of 450 kinds of fish on sale is unparalleled. The action starts early, though the 5.40a.m auction of monster-size *maguro* (tuna), some weighing as much as 300 kg, is now held behind closed doors. Get there by 8 a.m., however, and you will witness the extraordinary hustle and bustle of the market in full swing. As a bonus, after things have quietened down you can join the market professionals for a unique breakfast at one of the Tsukiji sushi bars, where the fish, naturally, is as fresh as can be.

A Shinto priest wears a white silk tunic, or *kariginu*, over a long divided skirt.

the station everyday and continued to do so for eleven years after his master's death in 1925, an expression of canine fidelity that is highly respected in Japan.

Harajuku

A kilometre north of Shibuya, Harajuku is a favourite haunt of Tokyo teenagers, who come here on Sundays to hang out and look cool in Yoyogi Park and, for girls, to stand on Jingu-bashi in front of the entrance to the Meiji Shrine dressed in outrageous Goth clothes or period Victoriana and be photographed by tourists. Takeshita-dori is where they come to shop, an alley lined with stalls selling coloured glasses, outlandish fashions and biker clothing at bargain prices.

Meiji Shrine

Set in a beautiful wooded park, the Meiji Shrine is the national focus of the Shinto religion, where people come to mark significant stages of their lives: newly-weds come to have their marriages blessed; parents bring babies dressed in their best or write out prayers for their children's success in exams. The shrine was built in 1920 and dedicated to the Emperor Meiji, whose reign (1868–1912) saw the transformation of Japan from a medieval to a modern state. It was destroyed by World War II bombs and rebuilt in 1958. Around the shrine, more than 100,000 seedlings sent from all over the country have grown into a forest.

The Treasure Museum at the northern end of the park displays relics of the emperor and his consort Empress Shoken. Be sure also to visit the Meiji-jingu Garden, which is especially noted for its displays of irises in June.

Omote-sando-dori

Leading southeast from Harajuku, Omote-sando is a broad avenue packed with top designer shops, from Prada and Dolce & Gabbana to Burberry and Louis Vuitton. In the tangle of small streets behind Omote-sando is a host of small, individual and extremely chic boutiques.

Ota Museum

Just off the Harajuku end of Omote-sando, the museum houses a superb collection of Edo-era *ukiyo-e*, woodblock prints, displayed in changing exhibitions.

Shinjuku

A cluster of shining skyscrapers to the north of Harajuku marks the business and hotel district of Shinjuku. The old gateway to Tokyo from the west, it had always specialized in welcoming weary travellers. Then the coming of the railways gave it a boost, and Kabuki-cho near the station became Japan's biggest red light area. It's still a centre for nightlife and low life, from excellent restaurants to massage parlours, bars and clubs where the entertainment tests the limits of legality.

By day or night, head for the twin-towered modernistic extravaganza of the Tokyo Metropolitan Government Office, which is signposted from Shinjuku Station. Ear-popping express lifts zoom you up to the 45th floor for amazing views of the city that extend as far as Mt Fuji 100 km away. You can visit both towers, which have souvenir shops and cafés at the top and are open from 9.30 a.m. to 11 p.m., with the night-time views being even more spectacular.

Yokohama

On the southwest side of Tokyo Bay, Yokohama developed rapidly after the Meiji Restoration, when it became one of the few designated places where foreigners could live and trade. It is now Japan's second-largest city and serves as the deepwater port for Tokyo. The two are only 30 km (19 miles) apart and linked by modern road and rail networks, yet Yokohama feels very different from its great neighbour to the north. Though the population is more than 3.6 million, most of the city is scaled far below skyscraper level, with whole neighbourhoods of small family shops and houses and some of the country's most attractive suburbs, and there's an agreeable harbourfront park, backed by modern hotels, office buildings and department stores.

Along the waterfront

Located in the fast-developing northwest district, the Minato Mirai 21 complex is dominated by the Landmark Tower, at 305 m the tallest building in Japan and containing the world's fastest elevator. The views from the Landmark Tower Sky Garden, 69 stories up, are magnificent. There are two good museums near here. Behind the tower is the entertainingly hands-on Mitsubishi Minato Mirai Industrial Museum, while a short walk towards the harbour brings you to the Yokohama Maritime Museum. On a spit of land in the bay itself, Cosmo World is an amusement park with one of the world's biggest Ferris wheels.

Called the Bund, the original waterfront has been planted with trees and flowers and embellished with fountains and statues to create the harbourside Yamashita Park. Moored next to the park is the old passenger liner *Hikawa Maru*, now open to the public with several on-board restaurants and a summertime beer garden.

At the north end of the park, the Silk Centre building contains the tourist information office and the Silk Museum, where you can learn all about the art of producing the shimmering fabric, from raising silkworms to unravelling, spinning and weaving the thread.

At the opposite end of Yamashita Park, Marine Tower, 106 m high, was built from the debris of the 1923 earthquake. Apart from its role as lighthouse and municipal trademark, it provides panoramic observatory platforms, a marine museum and a restaurant, not to mention souvenirs galore.

Chinatown

A few minutes walk inland from the harbourfront is Yokohama's Chinatown, with red paper lanterns garlanding the crowded streets, garish designs on the shopfronts, and a happy abundance of Chinese restaurants. The Yokohama Daisekai has eight floors of restaurants, shops and a theatre that puts on Chinese operas and other shows.

Nearby Yokohama Stadium is home of the Taiyo Whales baseball team. Baseball has become the most popular national sport, and it's well worth checking out a match if you have the time.

Sankei-en

On the southeastern outskirts of the city, the delightful Sankei-en

See the bright lights of Yokohama from its giant ferris wheel.

garden was devised by a 19th-century silk tycoon and opened to the public in 1906. Among 17 ha (42 acres) of babbling brooks, flowering trees, lotus ponds and temples, the calm is disturbed only by the cawing of crows and the chattering of tour groups following their flag-bearers. Nine buildings here are officially listed as important cultural relics, notably a 15th-century three-storey pagoda moved from Kyoto and the Rinshun-kaku, an authentic feudal villa in an idyllic pondside setting.

Kamakura

This delightful little coastal town close to Sagami Bay, around 50 km south of Yokohama, holds a historic and cultural position in Japanese life way beyond its size. At the end of the 12th century it became the centre of the Minamoto shogunate and effectively the capital of Japan until Emperor Go-Daigo reclaimed power for the imperial court in Kyoto in 1333. As a result, there are around 65 temples in the area, the most famous of them housing the Daibutsu, or Great Buddha. Nowadays Kamakura is popular with day-tripping Tokyoites, who come here to enjoy a slice of Japanese history and a walk on the beach.

The Temples

A clutch of interesting Zen Buddhist temples stand north of Kamakura town centre—you can get off the train at Kita-Kamakura station to reach them more easily.

Engakuji is a few hundred metres east of the station. The temple was founded in 1282 by Tokimune Hojo, probably to commemorate the soldiers killed during the failed Mongolian invasion a year earlier. Look out for the huge temple bell, dating from 1301.

A short distance south of here, across the railway line, Tokeiji was known during the Tokugawa shogunate as a refuge for women who had left their husbands—those who were caught before making it to the temple grounds faced severe punishment or even execution.

The nearby Jochiji, founded in 1283, is another attractive Zen temple with particularly fine

Two impressive statues of Buddha. Standing 15 m tall, the Daibutsu (Great Buddha) at the **Todaiji temple** in **Nara** is the world's largest bronze statue. The 13th-century Daibutsu at **Kamakura** is a mere 13.35 m in height, but makes up for it by being the more beautiful of the two.

Rainer Hackenberg

grounds. From here you can continue to Kenchoji, the oldest Zen temple in Japan (with a lovely Zen garden behind the main hall), or pick up an enjoyable 3-km trail across the wooded hill to Kamakura's most famous sight, the Daibutsu, in Kotokuin temple.

Daibutsu
The Daibutsu is a beautiful bronze statue of a seated Buddha tilting slightly forward, 13.35 m high. It was cast in 1252 and was originally housed in a wooden structure. This was washed away in a massive tsunami that hit Kamakura in 1498; the Buddha has been out in the open ever since. The statue faces towards the sea, which is only a ten-minute walk away and a great place to unwind after a hard morning's temple-viewing.

Nikko
"Do not say *kekko* (magnificent) until you've seen Nikko," goes an old Japanese proverb. There has been a Shinto shrine in the town, around 100 km north of Tokyo, since the 4th century and Buddhist temples since the 8th, but it's the extraordinary Toshogu Shrine, the burial place of the first Tokugawa shogun, that gives the proverb its real meaning. Beyond the town, Nikko National Park has several areas of natural beauty to discover.

Toshogu Shrine
A Shinto stone *torii* (gate) and a Buddhist five-storey pagoda mark the entrance to this opulently decorated complex of buildings begun in 1634 by Tokugawa Iemitsu as a mausoleum for his grandfather, Tokugawa Ieyasu. Carry on through the Omotemon, with its seated protective gate-figures, to the *Shinkyusha* (Sacred Stable). This houses the imperial white horses but is famous for its allegorical lintel decoration of three wise monkeys in the pose of "hear no evil, speak no evil, see no evil."

In the Yakushi-doh, a hall behind the drum tower, see the Nakuruyu, a dragon painted on the ceiling: when clappers are struck beneath it, the dragon seems to make a crying sound.

The Yomei-mon is the most lavish of the shrine's buildings. It's covered in red lacquerwork and gold leaf and decorated with paintings of animals, flowers and dancing girls. Check out Nemurineko, a well-known wooden figure of a sleeping cat to the right of Yomei-mon, before continuing to the cedar-lined path leading up to Tokugawa Ieyasu's tomb.

Daiyuin Mausoleum
Set within a fine grove of Japanese cedar trees a few hundred meters west of Toshogu, this ornate shrine is dedicated to Ie-

Mount Fuji likes to play hide-and-seek with the clouds and mist.

mitsu, the third of the Tokugawa shoguns, who died in 1651. The layout of the buildings is similar—though smaller in scale—to its more famous neighbour.

Rinnoji

Nikko's most important Buddhist temple is just south of Toshogu. It was founded in the 8th century by Shodo Shonin, the monk who first brought Buddhism to this region. Its main building, the Sanbutsudo (Three Buddha Hall) has three large, gold-lacquered wooden statues of the Buddha, including the impressive 1000-armed Senju Kannon.

Opposite the Sanbutsudo, the temple's treasure hall has an adjacent Japanese garden.

Nikko National Park

The national park covers some 1400 sq km of mountainous terrain, dominated by the extinct volcano of Mt Nantai, 2,482 m high. The scenic Lake Chuzenji lies 10 km west of Nikko, where you'll also find the powerful Kegon Waterfalls, at 99 m the highest in Japan.

While you're in Nikko, be sure to pick up a map at the tourist office, as there are lots of good walking trails around the park. After a long hike you can relax in one of the area's many *onsen*, baths formed from hot mineral springs.

Mount Fuji

At 3,776 m, Fuji-san, as it's always called in Japan, is the highest peak in the country, and its perfect conical outline has become the classic symbol of the nation. It's located about 100 km to the west of Tokyo and takes some 2 hours to get by train from the city. Snow-capped for three-quarters of the year, it's climbable by even moderately fit hikers during the summer months and even as late as October—though the Japanese mainly keep to July and August.

There are ten stations on the way up, with a road reaching as far as the fifth one. The ascent from here takes around 4–5 hours. The most popular time to be on the peak is at sunrise when there's less chance of it being shrouded in mist. Seeing the rising sun from this extraordinary vantage point is, perhaps, the quintessential Japanese experience. To do this, of course, you either have to climb Fuji at night, or go up in the afternoon and stay at a mountain hut close to the top. Either way, bear in mind that it is always cold at the top at night and early morning, and weather conditions can change in minutes, so be sure to bring appropriate clothing and provisions.

For a more relaxed close-up of Fuji, head to Fuji-Go-ko (Fuji Five Lakes) on the north side,

Mt Fuji's hot springs can boil eggs and dye them, too.

with hiking trails, old temples, lava caves and spectacular views of the mountain. Great views are also to be had further away in the hot-spring resort area of Hakone. The vista is particularly lovely from the pleasure boats that ply the calm waters of Lake Ashi. From Hakone, a little train takes you to Gora, where you can catch a cable car and ropeway to Togendai on the lake shore. Boats link Moto-Hakone with Hakone-Machi on the other side of the lake. Make a stop at Owakudani, which affords a wonderful view of Fuji, and stroll along the path among the fumeroles and sulphurous pools. You might like to sample *kuro-tamago*, black eggs, hard-boiled in the steaming water; each one you eat will add seven years to your life. They taste just like ordinary hard-boiled eggs.

Northern Honshu

North from Tokyo, and readily accessible by train or road, is some of Japan's loveliest rural scenery, such as Matsushima, rated one of the nation's three most beautiful places, and historic towns, like the samurai settlement at Kakunodate. It's also a mountainous area of hot springs and cooler climes—a perfect combination for making the most of hiking and other outdoor pursuits.

Matsushima

Not far from Sendai, a large city two hours northeast of Tokyo by Shinkansen, the bay resort of Matsushima is justifiably famous as an area of great natural beauty, though this also means that it gets extremely crowded with tourists, especially at weekends and holidays.

The bay is dotted with around 250 pine-clad islands, sculpted into an amazing array of different formations by the waves. The nearest ones, O-shima and Fukuura-jima, are connected to the mainland by bridges and make for a very pleasant stroll. The best way to see the others is by taking a cruise boat from Matsushima Kaigan Pier at the harbour.

The town has a few interesting sights of its own. In feudal times the region was under the sway of the Date family. Zuiganji, a temple 200 m back from the harbour, was built in 1606 by the best-known of the clan, Masamune Date. A teahouse, Kanran-tei, was a gift to the Dates by Toyotomi Hideyoshi in the 16th century; it was set by the waterside, where they could enjoy the ocean view as they sipped.

Chusonji

Just outside Hiraizumi, around 100 km north of Sendai, this extraordinary temple was part of a 12th-century project by the Fujiwara clan to establish its own version of Kyoto. Most of the grand buildings were destroyed in the civil war that led to the establishment of the Minamoto shogunate in the 1180s, but Chusonji survived. It dates from 1109 and is reached along a steep avenue with superb views over the valley. Ornately decorated in black laquerwork, gold and mother-of-pearl, the Konjikido (Golden Hall) is a striking sight. The temple treasury houses various artefacts relating to the Fujiwara.

Kakunodate

Around 150 km north of Hiraizumi, Kakunodate is a mountain castle town, founded by the Satake clan from Kyoto in the 17th century. They built the samurai houses that are still intact today, and brought with them the cherry trees that are planted along the Hinokinai River and in the gardens of their houses (the town is now known for its cherrywood craft items).

Located in the Uchimachi, or Inner Town, the samurai houses are among the finest in Japan, and are open to the public as museums. The main museum is in the Aoyagi-ke, with an eclectic display of exhibits on the samurai family who lived there, while the Denshokan house has examples of *kabazaiku*, or cherrywood carvings.

Towada-Hachimantai National Park

At the heart of the park, towards Honshu's northern tip, lies Lake Towada, occupying a vast mountaintop crater more than 300 m deep. The area is filled with *onsen* and thermal resorts for relaxation: a great way to earn a hot bath is to follow the 14-km Oirase Valley trail, starting from the eastern shore of the lake and leading through a gorge with thick woodland, waterfalls and excellent views.

Zen garden at Kyoto's Ryoanji—for contemplation and meditation.

Kyoto and Kansai region

If you want to experience the essence of Japanese culture, you need to visit its historic heartland. The Kansai region was the mainspring of Japanese nationhood. Following Japan's unification at the end of the 4th century, magnificent imperial courts were established, with the first permanent court at Nara, and then at Kyoto, which remained the capital city until 1868.

Meanwhile, the country's exposure to foreign lands—which has always been a complex issue for the Japanese—came through the great ports of Osaka and Kobe, through which Chinese and Korean culture arrived at the court. Later, in the 19th century, Western trading posts were allowed in Kobe, as Japan was thrust into its own remarkable industrial revolution. Today, the main cities of the region offer a chance to see all sides of the modern nation, and with a superb transport system it's only a short ride between the cultural and religious shrines of Nara and Kyoto, the vital metropolis of Osaka and Kobe's port.

Kyoto City Centre
Busy with traffic and bustling with modern city life, downtown Kyoto might not immediately strike you as the epitome of traditional culture. It's also surprisingly big, and you'll need a pair of good walking shoes if you intend to travel on foot between the sights. However, one of the delights of wandering through its streets is the tendency to happen upon areas of great charm when you least expect it. There's also the additional bonus that thanks to its regular, grid-system layout, and the landmark Kyoto Tower giving a point of reference to the south of the centre, it's always easy to find your way around.

Imperial Palace
Occupying a substantial chunk of central Kyoto, the Imperial Palace has stood on this site since 794, though the vulnerable wooden buildings burned down numerous times before the latest, 19th-century reconstruction. The slim spires above the thatched roofs of the Imperial Palace are in fact lightning rods. Although the imperial court left Kyoto for Tokyo soon after this version was completed, new emperors are still enthroned here.

Everything about the palace is exceptional, the architecture, interior decoration and, most notably, the 300-year-old garden. In Japan the great landscape gardeners are listed high in the credits, like architects in the West. Guided visits are compulsory; permits

IMPERIAL CITY

Japan's emperors lived in Kyoto for more than a thousand years, and the city remains the nation's spiritual centre, a place where tradition and beauty flourish. This is in part because despite enduring the ravages of civil wars and major fires over the centuries, it's one of the few cities to have survived World War II intact: Allied bombers were ordered not to destroy this ancient cultural treasure.

The city was laid out in the 8th century as a chequerboard grid based on the Tang capital of Ch'ang-an in China. Although the downtown area is as built-up as any in the land—this is a major city of 1.5 million people, after all—its atmospheric hillsides, rivers and canals, historic temples and imperial palace transcend all modern impositions. Kyoto is still a place where you can turn a corner and find yourself suddenly in a timeless street where the old wooden houses have discreet latticed windows, where geishas and other ladies in kimonos walk elegantly on their way, and the smell of incense and the sound of temple bells drift in the air.

Rainer Hackenberg

must be obtained with a passport 20 minutes before the 10 a.m. or 2 p.m. tours.

Nijo Castle
Built at the beginning of the 17th century by Shogun Tokugawa Ieyasu to defend the Imperial Palace a kilometre to the northeast, as well as to show the emperor who was boss—the castle is protected by a moat in which multicoloured carp compete with swans for tourist handouts.

Enter through the opulent Kara-mon. As in the temples and shrines, you have to take off your shoes before walking through the castle's corridors. Once inside, you'll be treated to a series of lavish 17th-century screen paintings of tigers, hawks, cherry blossom and misty mountain scenery by renowned artists such as Tanyu Kano. Notice the squeak underfoot: the so-called "nightingale floor" was designed to betray intruders.

Before leaving, head round to the Ninomaru Palace Garden, a traditional Japanese garden set around a lake with three rock islands designed by the celebrated landscape artist Kobori Enshu (1579–1647).

Nishiki Market
From the castle, strike out due east along Oike-dori, turning right onto Kawaramachi-dori, the long and very lively shopping street that runs north–south through the heart of downtown Kyoto. After five blocks, turn left to this superb covered food market known locally as "Kyoto's Kitchen". With everything from seaweed to soya beans on sale, it's always busy and a great way to see the citizens of Kyoto involved in one of their favourite pursuits. Most of the surrounding streets are also covered and are full of souvenir shops and restaurants.

Ponto-cho
Continue eastwards, where this narrow street runs between Sanjo-dori and Shijo-dori just before they arrive at the River Kamo. Lined with tiny traditional houses, most of them converted into bars and restaurants, it's extremely atmospheric in the evening, when the lanterns are lit and there's a good chance of seeing a geisha hurrying along.

East Kyoto
The eastern side of the River Kamo is home to some of the city's most intriguing districts, such as the entertainment quarter of Gion, famous for its geisha teahouses. This part of Kyoto also contains a range of good museums and, in the Higashiyama-ku (Eastern Hills), a number of ancient and highly scenic temples.

The roofs of Kiyomizu peep out from an ocean of pink blossom.

Sanjusangendo

Southeast of the centre, a short distance from Shichijo Bridge, this extraordinary temple is famous for its 1,001 statues of Kannon, the Goddess of Mercy. The central figure, a gilded statue of the Kannon Bodhisattva over 3.3 m tall, has 11 faces on the crown of its head and "1000" arms (really only 40, but they say that each one saved 25 worlds) wielding bells, wheels and lotus flowers. It is officially classified as a national treasure and is about 700 years old, as is the almost overwhelming golden army surrounding it; each of the 1,000 life-size statues is slightly different in detail.

Kyoto National Museum

The National Museum, opposite Sanjusangendo, displays its collections of Japanese sculpture and paintings in rotation so you can never be sure what you will see. The priceless works have been gathered from the temples and palaces of Kyoto, Nara and other cultural centres and also include weapons and armour, period costumes and masks from the *noh* theatre.

Kiyomizu-dera

Kiyomizu, a little over a kilometre northeast of the museum on Higashiyama-ku, is one of the most famous of Kyoto's temples. It's a rare feat of 17th-century engineering, hanging out over a canyon with the help of 139 wooden pillars and offering magnificent views of Kyoto. Women have come to this spot for more than a thousand years to pray for easy childbirth. However, it's also known as a place for unhappy lovers to jump from, the phrase "to take a Kiyomizu leap" being proverbial in Japan for making any momentous decision.

On the long hike up to the temple, fascinating shopping possibilities unfold. Model pagodas, samurai swords, silk and ceramics can all be bought at the numerous craft stalls perched on the side of the hill. On the way down, make a detour to the right to charming Kiyomizuzaka, an attractive old street with smart cafés and souvenir shops and a view over the picturesque Yasaka Pagoda.

Museums

A few kilometres to the north, the National Museum of Modern Art houses a highly rated collection of modern Japanese paintings and prints, ceramics, jewellery, sculpture, textiles, and so on, shown on a rotating basis.

Located opposite it, the Municipal Museum of Art displays works by 20th-century Japanese artists, many of whom came from or were based in Kyoto.

DREAMS OF THE GEISHA

Nothing evokes the image of the Floating World more powerfully than the geisha. These enigmatic figures from another age, dressed in richly embroidered kimonos and with expressionless chalk-white faces, can still be seen around the sidestreets of Kyoto's Gion district and Ponto-cho just across the river. Geisha means "art person". They emerged under the Tokugawa Shogunate as a class of women who, as consummate singers, dancers and musicians, were set apart from ordinary courtesans and prostitutes, and entertained the nobility and the samurai. They are still famous for their skills at singing and dancing to the accompaniment of the samisen (a lute-like instrument), as well as for their ability to make witty conversation and offer subtle flattery to wealthy executives, as they once did to samurai warriors. Nowadays the geisha are becoming an endangered species. Before World War II there were more than 80,000: today there are fewer than 2000, most of them in Kyoto. Whatever your views on the relevance of the geisha in the modern world, the sight of one of them shuffling through the Gion area is to be treasured as a fleeting reminder of ancient Japan.

Agnès Curchod

Heian Shrine

You can see the great, red *torii* of the Heian Shrine from the plaza in front of the museums. Founded at the end of the 19th century to commemorate Kyoto's 1100th anniversary, this complex of buildings reproduces on a smaller scale Kyoto's first imperial palace of 794. The landscape garden is especially lovely when the cherry trees or irises are in bloom.

Path of Philosophy

Head back past the Municipal Museum of Art and turn left along the wide canal towards the foothills of Higashiyama and delightful Nanzenji temple. From here you can follow signposts in English to the beautiful Path of Philosophy *(Tetsugaku-no-michi)*, the favoured walking place of a professor at Kyoto University in the early 20th century. It's a haven of tranquillity, with the modern city hidden behind the trees and viewpoints artfully positioned to reveal only houses and temple rooftops and the mountains to the west. The walk takes around 40 minutes; on the way there are delightfully secluded temples, and some welcome cafés, to stop at.

Ginkakuji

The Path of Philosophy ends at Gingakuji (Temple of the Silver Pavilion), a country villa built in 1482 by the Shogun Yoshimasa Ashikaga as a counterpart to Kinkakuji (The Golden Pavilion) in northwest Kyoto. This one is far more restrained, because the funds ran out before it received its intended coating of silver. As compensation, it has one of Kyoto's finest Zen gardens, with dazzlingly white raked sand.

West Kyoto

This part of the city is rich in sightseeing opportunities, including world-famous temples and areas of spectacular beauty.

Kinkakuji

In the foothills of the mountains to the northwest of the city, Kinkakuji (Temple of the Golden Pavilion) was built in 1397 as a retirement villa for Shogun Yoshimitsu Ashikaga. The current three-storey pavilion is a replica of the original, which was burned down in 1950 by a young Buddhist monk (the subject of a fascinating novel by Japan's best-known modern writer, Yukio Mishima, 1925–40). However, the reconstruction is even more opulent, with the two upper storeys being completely covered in thick gold leaf. Topped by a bronze Chinese phoenix and sitting by a carp-filled lake in a beautifully landscaped garden, this is one of the great icons of Japanese culture.

The lanterns of Kasuga Taisha shrine make a great playground for Nara's deer.

Ryoanji

A 15-minute walk south of Kinkakuji, Ryoanji dates from the mid-15th century and is more famous for its extraordinary abstract Zen garden than its temple buildings. Here, you can sit on a raised platform overlooking the walled, rectangular area of raked gravel, in which are set 15 large stones (only 14 of which can be seen at the same time from any given angle), and contemplate its meaning.

Arashiyama

Continue southwest to the picturesque hillside area of Arashiyama. Here you'll find the attractive Togetsu-kyo Bridge across the Katsura River looking like a vision of old Kyoto, while banked up on the hill behind it is an artfully arranged forest, designed to blaze with maples in November and uplift the spirit with cherry blossom in April. Tenryuji temple was founded in 1339 on the site of Emperor Go-Daigo's villa and is, like Ryoanji, part of the Rinzai school of Zen. Its magnificent garden is laid out with ponds in the interlocking form of yin and yang, and has a stunning display of maple trees.

South Kyoto

Just 5 minutes by train from the centre, the Fushimi-Inari Taisha is a Shinto shrine devoted to the god (or goddess) of fertility and industry. Founded in the 8th century, the shrine features a tunnel winding for 4 km up the slope of Mt Inari, made of thousands of red *torii* donated by worshippers. Among them sit statues of the fox messengers, *kitsune*, many holding between their jaws the key to a rice granary.

Nara

The first imperial city of Nara hangs onto much of its ancient culture and charm. It was established as Japan's capital in 710, and over the 84 years of the "Nara period" the spirit of Japanese culture was forged, with Buddhism flowering as a national religion. Nearby Horyuji predates Nara by more than a century, and makes for a fascinating side trip from the city.

The historic district is on the east side of town. Most of its temples and shrines, and a good museum, are enclosed within Nara Park, whose extra attraction is a herd of over 1,000 deer, as tame as lapdogs and who come tugging at your clothes and bags. A trumpet calls them home to their pen at sunset.

Kofukuji

At the entrance to Nara Park, the temple was founded in 710 and once contained more than 150 buildings. None of the 8th-century originals exist today. The five-storey pagoda dates from the 15th century and, dreamily reflected in Sarusawa Pond just to the south, is now the defining image of the city.

Nara National Museum

The two buildings of the Nara National Museum are a short distance east of the temple and offer a concentrated dose of ancient Buddhist art. The West Gallery dates from 1895 and displays historic statues of Buddha, while the newer East Gallery has paintings, calligraphy and sculptures from nearby temples shown in rotation.

Todaiji

After entering the park proper, you'll see to the left the temple's huge gate, Nandai-mon, beyond which are Nara's two biggest attractions—literally. First, you are confronted by the splendid Daibutsu-den hall. This is a 17th-century reconstruction at two-thirds the scale of the 8th-century original, yet it's still the world's largest wooden structure. It shelters the world's largest bronze statue: the Daibutsu, or Great Buddha. Cast in 746, it stands 15 m tall, with the ears alone measuring 2.5 m from tip to lobe.

Nigatsudo

From the exit to the temple, head left up the hill to this attractive pavilion, from whose open balcony you can obtain fine views of Nara Park and the Kofukuji pagoda rising above the treetops.

Kasuga Taisha

A hillside path leads to one of Nara's most beautiful spots. The shrine, set within a grove at the foot of cedar-clad Mt Kasuga, was founded in 768 by the powerful Fujiwara family and dedicated to four Shinto deities. The main building has a marvellous colonnade of vermilion columns and beams, while the paths in the woods around it and the long avenue at the entrance are lined with thousands of stone lanterns, while thousands more, in bronze, illuminate the interior. They are all lit at once for a festival in early February and mid August. The shrine was torn down and rebuilt every 20 years for many centuries; the custom was discontinued at the end of the Edo period.

Horyuji

About 10 km southwest of Nara, Horyuji is Japan's oldest surviving temple complex. Remarkably, parts of this building date from not long after its foundation in 607 by Prince Shotoku, who was responsible for making Japan a Buddhist nation—indeed the Kondo (Golden Hall) can claim to be the oldest wooden structure in the world.

Apart from the Kondo, Horyuji is dominated by a magnificent five-storey pagoda. However, this large site has several other places of great interest, such as the ancient central gate and cloister gallery and, in the east section of the temple, the exquisite Yumedono (Hall of Visions), an 8th-century octagonal pavilion containing a life-size sculpture of Prince Shotoku.

The modern temple gallery has a first-rate collection of treasures that date back across almost 1400 years. Among them are some fine 12th-century Heian-period masks and the Tamamushi Shrine from the Asuka period (mid-6th- early 8th centuries), which was once decorated in the iridescent colours of the tamamushi beetle's wings.

Osaka

From the mid-5th century till the 7th century, Osaka was the site of a Yamato palace complex, losing its importance when Nara became the permanent capital in 710. It subsequently benefited as the port city for the Kansai region and by the 16th century was vir-

Even though it's made of ferro-concrete, Osaka Castle makes a fine model for a schoolchildren's art class. | Shopping can be confusing when you can't read the signs!

tually a self-governing city-state run by its merchants. This came to an end with Oda Nobunaga's military unification of Japan in 1569, while in the Tokugawa era it was controlled directly by the shogunate. The city was largely destroyed during World War II, but has bounced back to become a major business and industrial powerhouse. Its 2.6 million inhabitants are famous for being no-nonsense and down-to-earth, with a passion for good food and drink. As a result it has some of the best cuisine and liveliest nightlife in the country.

Behind the slick, super-efficient façade of central Osaka you'll find several fine museums, ancient temples and beautiful traditional gardens. The centre is laid out in a grid system, with the mega shopping and transport hub of Umeda to the north, and the relative calm of Tennoji to the south.

Umeda Sky Building

A short walk west of Umeda Station, the space-age Sky Building has a 173-m-high open observation deck with unparalleled views over Osaka. It's a great place for watching the sunset behind Osaka Bay or the downtown area lit at night. There's a bar on the 40th floor, while the basement has a restaurant mall in the style of a pre-war Showa-era street.

Museum of Oriental Ceramics

The museum is located around a kilometre south of Umeda station on Nakanoshima, an island in the Yodo River containing most of the city's municipal buildings, including the town hall. It has a first-rate collection of ancient artefacts that come mainly from China and Korea. The peaceful park at the eastern tip of the island is a good place for a photo of Osaka Castle.

Mint Museum

The big building on the west bank of the Yodo, facing Sakuranomiya Park, is the Mint. Osakans are notoriously commercial-minded, and a popular greeting in Osaka dialect translates as "Are you making any money?" If you make an appointment at the Mint 10 days in advance, you can watch them doing this literally, right before your very eyes. Otherwise, you might like to visit the museum, whose exhibits are devoted to Japanese and foreign coinage. At cherry blossom time, the citizens of Osaka throng to the museum park to contemplate the delicate clouds of pink and white flowers, special here because they are double-petalled.

Fujita Art Museum

In the eastern part of Sakuranomiya Park, the house of the painter Fujita (1886–1968) has

Three fabulous castles. The splendid 16th-century castle at **Himeji** is nicknamed the White Egret and universally acclaimed as the finest of Japan's surviving original castles. **Osaka Castle**, an imposing ferro-concrete reconstruction of the 1930s, has great views of the city and a museum of samurai costumes. The delightful Edo-era hilltop castle at **Matsuyama**, on Shikoku, sits in a magnificent grove of cedar trees.

been converted into the Fujita Art Museum, with collections covering Chinese and Japanese painting from the 11th century to the present day, ceramics, and a variety of objects pertaining to the tea ceremony.

Osaka Castle

The 16th-century warlord Toyotomi Hideyoshi, with a little help from a workforce of more than 30,000 men, built the first gigantic Osaka Castle: this was destroyed a few decades later in 1615 when his successor, Tokugawa Ieyesu, crushed a local rebellion. It was rebuilt, yet again destroyed by Ieyesu's descendants in the 1860s during their overthrow at the time of the Meiji Restoration.

Standing just south of Sakuranomiya Park, the current version is a 1931 ferro-concrete replica of the 42-m high keep. After its recent facelift it looks as spectacular as any of Japan's genuine old castles. It's protected by a complex of lake-sized moats and enormous ramparts that include parts of the original walls. You can take a lift up to the top floor for a splendid view of the city. The castle museum houses an interesting collection of weapons, armour, period costumes and historical documents illustrating the Hideyoshi era. The castle garden, meanwhile, is Osaka's best-known spot for cherry blossom viewing in April.

Osaka Museum of History

This modern, oval-shaped building near the castle is devoted to the history and culture of Osaka, with life-size reconstructions, scale models, photographs and film. There are useful explanations in English, and great views of Osaka Castle from the museum's top floor.

Minami district

For a glimpse of Osaka as its most vibrant, stroll around the district known as Minami, at the heart of the old merchant town west of the castle. It takes in downtown Namba and the bustling Dotonburi canal area, its

Close-up view of the cherry blossom in Osaka's castle garden.

narrow streets lined with restaurants, shops and bars, teeming with life day and night. Here, on Dotonbori itself, is the National Bunraku Theatre; Osaka has been home to this colourful puppet drama since the 17th century.

City Art Museum
Located in Tennoji Park, south of Namba, the City Art Museum houses the renowned Abe collection consisting of some 200 Chinese paintings of the 9th to 13th centuries, as well as ceramics from the Ming and Ching dynasties. The park also has a zoo, botanical garden and outdoor karaoke sessions on Sunday.

Shitennoji
Across busy Tanimachi-suji Avenue, this is said to be the oldest Buddhist temple in Japan. It was founded in 593 but has been ravaged over and over again by wars and fires; the present complex, beautifully restored, includes a five-storey pagoda, a main hall and a lecture hall. The 13th-century *torii* is considered to be the oldest of its kind in the country.

Osaka Aquarium
Near Osaka Port, the aquarium claims to contain the world's biggest tank, inhabited by an enormous whale shark among other large fish.

Universal Studios Japan
Out towards Osaka Bay, Universal Studios Japan is, like its American counterparts, a lively theme park with superb rides based around cinematic themes, and a surefire winner with the kids.

Kobe
Reached in under 15 minutes from Osaka by Shinkansen train, Kobe is one of Japan's most cosmopolitan cities, something that began with its trade connections with China and Korea in the 8th century and continued in the 19th century when Westerners were allowed to live here. It was devastated by a major earthquake in January 1995, which killed more than 5000 people and caused huge damage to the city's housing and port facilities. The recovery has been remarkably swift, however, and Kobe today has regained its relaxed, international atmosphere.

Port area
As Japan's second-largest trading port, Kobe is rich in maritime sights: crowds of tankers, car-ferries, hydrofoils, container ships, freighters from Monrovia or Vladivostok, a black submarine flying the flag with the rising sun.

For a view over the harbour and the city, go up to the revolving observation platform on the

Port Tower, at Naka Pier. Kobe's lively Chinatown is located in the streets behind Naka Pier and is packed with bright red lanterns and Chinese restaurants.

To see things up close, catch one of the boats leaving for harbour round-trips from Meriken-Hatoba Pier, next to Naka Pier. In Meriken Park itself, the striking ship-like Kobe Maritime Museum provides a background to the city's nautical life. Near here is the Port of Kobe Earthquake Memorial Park, with a piece of a concrete pier smashed in the 1995 disaster.

On a man-made island in the harbour, Kobe looks to the future. Designed as a "cultural city on the sea", Port Island's industrial, housing and recreational areas are linked to the central business district by an overhead automated transport system. Recorded voices call out the stations in Japanese and American-accented English. The island boasts a landscaped garden, a sports centre, and a theme park featuring flowers and birds.

Kobe City Museum

Just back from the port, the Kobe City Museum looks at the history of the city up to and including the terrible 1995 earthquake. But pride of place goes to the priceless collection of 16th- and 17th century Namban art. Namban was the word given to the earliest Europeans (or "southern Barbarians") to arrive here, and these amazing paintings, screens and prints depicting the Portuguese in their baggy trousers, with their strange weapons, reveal the first traces of foreign influence on Japanese artists.

Kitano

Foreigners were first allowed to live in Kobe during the Victorian era, and were mostly involved in commerce; the numbers are now in the tens of thousands. Japanese tourists, who find this cosmopolitanism fascinating, flock to the Kitano district where a few dozen rather garish European-style, 19th-century houses are preserved. From here you can also take the Shin-Kobe Cable Car 400 m up to the mountain overlooking Kobe for excellent views of the city and the bay.

Himeji

Located 75 km west of Osaka in Hyogo Prefecture, Himeji developed during the 14th century as a fortress town. Today, it's still primarily known for its five-storey castle. This was constructed in about 1600 by the feudal lord Ikeda Terumasa and is a rare survivor from the past—most Japanese castles were destroyed either during the Meiji Restoration at the end of the 19th century or in

World War II. Especially noteworthy are its beautiful curving rooftops. Thought to resemble birds in flight, they earned the castle the name *Shirasagi*, or White Egret Castle. At the top of an intricate set of paths, designed to hamper the progress of an attacking army, is the Daitenshu, or Main Keep. This has superb views over the town and as far as the Inland Sea. Look for the Oki-ku-ido Well, said to be haunted by the voice of a servant girl who was tortured to death after being falsely accused of stealing a valuable plate.

Himeji's other main sights are situated near the castle. Just west of it is the Himeji Koko-en, a landscaped garden. Laid out in 1992, it contains teahouses, picturesque rockeries and carp-filled ponds. To the north of the castle, in a building designed by one of Japan's leading modernist architects, Tange Kenzo, the Hyogo Prefectural History Museum contains a fascinating display of models, plans and other items related to Japan's great castles. You can also don a suit of samurai armour or, if you prefer, a 12-layered court kimono.

Awash in the golden light of the setting sun, the White Egret Castle in Himeji with its curving roofs. | A pampered pet taken for a ride.

The huge *torii* at Miyajima has come to symbolize Japan itself.

Western Honshu

The western part of Honshu is known as Chugoku, the "middle country". This harks back to a time when the region was at the geographical centre of Japanese civilization, the midway point between the imperial capital at Kyoto and the fertile island of Kyushu. It's now served by Bullet trains, and even the smallest towns are packed with brand new shopping malls gleaming with the latest in high-tech electronics and computer games. But alongside this you'll find glimpses of an ancient world of temples, castles and gardens, and magical offshore islands.

Bizen

Around 50 km west of Himeji, the town is home to the renowned Bizen-yaki unglazed pottery, made using a 1000-year-old technique. The patterning is created by the natural effects of the firing process. Centuries ago it became popular with tea masters for use in the Zen-inspired tea ceremony. The kilns are fuelled by wood, and their brick chimneys can be seen all around the town. Many of them have shops on site where you can buy the finished product—some even allow you to make your own piece of Bizen pottery. But the best place to get an overview of this ancient art is at the Bizen Pottery Traditional and Contemporary Art Museum, near the railway station. Here, modern ceramic work is placed in its context within the history and practice of Bizen pottery-making.

Okayama City

A further 30 km east of Bizen, this prefectural capital is famed throughout Japan for containing one of the country's best gardens. The Koraku-en was founded in 1686, and is packed with classic features found in all good Japanese parks such as artificial hills, lakes, islands and the obligatory teahouse—but this one is specially prized by the Japanese because of its large expanses of open lawn.

From Koraku-en, cross the Asahi river via Tsukimibashi bridge a little to the south and you'll arrive at Okayama Castle. It may look traditional, but it's a modern ferro-concrete reconstruction of the original, which was built in 1573 and destroyed under the Meiji Restoration. The black façade of the castle has earned it the nickname of U-jo, or Crow Castle, a typically down-to-earth Okayaman riposte to the more glamorous "White Egret" at Himeji.

Head northwards to the Okayama Prefectural Museum of Art. This puts on temporary exhibitions of art, and also has a permanent display of Bizen pottery and a fine collection of 15th-century ink paintings by Sesshu Toyo.

Kurashiki

Kurashiki lies just 26 km west of Okayama, and the urban sprawl of both cities means they almost merge into one other. At the heart of Kurashiki, though, is a beautifully preserved old town, with several Edo-period storehouses (known as *kura*) and merchants' homes, built between the 17th and the 19th centuries when this was the centre of the region's lucrative rice trade. Set around a tree-lined canal, along which the rice was transported, many of these historic buildings have now been turned into museums.

Across Imabashi, a bridge with distinctive stone dragons, the Ohara Museum of Art is made up of four different parts. Founded in the 1930s by the textile manufacturer Ohara Magosaburo, the neoclassical main gallery contains one of the best collections of Western art in Japan. It was largely put together in Europe in the decade after World War I, when Ohara's agent went on a spending spree, snapping up both Old Masters and the contemporary avant garde. As a result, major artists on display here range from El Greco to Van Gogh, Rodin and Picasso. More recent acquisitions have brought in the likes of Jackson Pollock, Warhol and Christo.

Of equal interest is the adjacent Craft Gallery, with a superb group of mainly ceramic works by the leading potters of the mid-20th century Japanese Folk Arts movement, such as Hamada Shoji and the British-born Bernard Leach. You will also find two other galleries, one devoted to modern Japanese art and the other to East Asian art, concentrating mainly on items from China.

Hiroshima

Stretched across a series of islands in the Ota River delta, Hiroshima (literally "wide island") was established as a castle town in the 16th century and remained a military centre after the Meiji Restoration. On August 6, 1945, it became the first city in the world to be struck by an atomic bomb. The bomb killed up to 80,000 people, though the aftereffects of radiation have added tens of thousands to the toll. Hiroshima was restored as a typical, modern Japanese city, and the main reason to go there today is to visit the museum and memorials devoted to that terrible event.

The main memorials associated with the blast are located in and around Peace Memorial Park, on a small wedge of land between the Ota and Motoyasu rivers, around 3 km west of Hiroshima JR Station. A streetcar goes from the station to the A-Bomb Dome *(Genbaku Domumae)*.

A-Bomb Dome

The bombed-out shell of the 1930s Industrial Promotion Hall, renamed the A-Bomb Dome, stands by the Motoyasu River. The building has been left as it was immediately after the blast to serve as a poignant symbol of the destruction of Hiroshima.

Peace Memorial Park

Just across the river, the park (*Heiwa-koen*) contains several memorials, including the Children's Peace Memorial, also known as the Tower of a Thousand Cranes, in honour of a schoolgirl, Sadako Sasaki, who died of leukaemia 10 years after the bombing and who vowed to make 1000 paper cranes in the hope she would get well before they were finished.

You will also see the Korean A-Bomb Memorial: a substantial percentage of the victims of the blast were Korean nationals brought to Japan as slave labour. The park's Memorial Ccnotaph carries the name of all those killed by the bomb. In front of it, the Peace Flame will remain burning till the last nuclear weapon has been abolished.

Rainer Hackenberg

Gardel/hemis.fr

The elegant lines of ceramics on display in Kurashiki's Craft Gallery. | In Hiroshima, the A-Bomb Dome has been left untouched.

Thousands of colourful paper cranes are brought to the Children's Peace Memorial every day.

Peace Memorial Museum

This important museum stands in the centre of the park, and has some very stark images of Hiroshima after the explosion. The 360° photograph of the city on display as you enter is a picture of total destruction; there are items stained with black rain, deeply unsettling photos of the effects of the bomb on its victims, and other graphic illustrations of the horror that descended upon the city that day. Part of the exhibition is devoted to the nuclear era.

Peace Memorial Hall

Close to the museum, the hall was designed by leading Japanese architect Tange Kenzo and opened in 2002. It's a hall of remembrance, displaying the names and photographs of the dead. It also raises the question of Japan's military brutality at the time, especially against civilians, a vital piece of background information lacking from the Peace Memorial Museum.

Miyajima

Just a couple of kilometres off the coast from Hiroshima, Miyajima boasts Japan's most famous image after Mt Fuji. It comes in the shape of the huge, red *torii* that at high tide seems to rise magically out of the sea in front of a shrine, Itsukushima-jinja. Try to be here at sunset, when light from the stone lanterns reflects off the water. It's not difficult to see why it has been officially designated one of the country's three most beautiful places.

The gate, 16 m high, was put here in 1875, though it's only the most recent in a line stretching back to 1168, when the temple was built by the warlord Taira no Kiyomori. Its position in the water signifies that the entire island is a Shinto shrine, and not merely the temple buildings.

At Itsukushima shrine is Japan's oldest *noh* theatre, dating from the 16th century. It's a supremely classical structure, but has one unusual feature: the stage juts into the sea, and the audience have to watch the play from the shore or on boats.

Miyajima would still be an attractive island even without its most famous feature. There's a population of tame deer that you'll find roaming along the beaches and among the temples, a forest that retains a hint of the mysterious, and a small mountain that gives great views of the Inland Sea. You can climb up Misen-san on foot in a couple of hours, though on one of Japan's hot summer days it might be easier to take the cable car. At the top is the Keizu no Reikado, a hall associated with the 9th-century Buddhist teacher Kobo Daishi.

It's said that the fire inside the hall has been kept alive for more than 1,100 years since it was first lit by Daishi himself.

Inland Sea

The most famous feature of Western Honshu will already have been visible from various high points along the coast. The Seto Naikai, or Inland Sea, comprises a spectacular series of channels dotted with hundreds of small islands that emerge from the often misty water like delicate brushstrokes in a classical Japanese painting.

Awaji-shima

The largest of the islands is at the eastern extremity of the Inland Sea's 440-km stretch of water. It was the epicentre of the 1995 Kobe earthquake, but has now largely recovered. Technology buffs will want to see the *Akashi Kaikyo Ohashi*, which links the island to Honshu and survived the earthquake relatively unharmed. At almost 4 km in length, this is the world's longest suspension bridge.

Shodo-shima

On the eastern side of the island is the magnificent Kanka-kei gorge, a 3-million-year old gash in the granite landscape. You can take a vertiginous cable-car ride above its fantastic rock formations; from the top you'll be treated to panoramic views of the Inland Sea. Most buses to Kanka-kei from the island's main port of Tonosho make a stop en route at Choshi-kei Monkey Park, which has a collection of apes from around the world.

At Shodo-shima's southern tip, the atmospheric old fishing village of Tanoura was the setting for one of Japan's best known anti-war novels, *Nijushi-no-Hitomi* (24 Eyes), by Sakae Tsuboi, and not far from here is a reconstruction of the village built for a film version of the novel made in the 1980s. The Eigamura film set, despite the prevalence of souvenir shops, still gives a good idea of how island life might have looked half a century ago.

Nao-shima

A short distance out to sea from the port of Uno, near Okayama, Nao-shima is the largest of a group of 27 small islands and boasts an unusual arts complex that also doubles as a hotel. Commissioned by the Benesse Corporation, the Benesse Island Naoshima Cultural Village is a little like finding a slice of Southern California that has somehow turned up in the Inland Sea. The gleaming white art gallery sits on a hill, and has great views of the surrounding islands. Inside are first-rate modern works by artists such as Giacometti, Hockney, Rauschenberg, Issey Miyake and Bruce Nauman.

Ikuchi-jima

This island is part of the Geiyo archipelago, once home to fierce pirates whose domination of the Inland Sea only came to an end in the late 16th century with the military victories of Japan's great unifier, Toyotomi Hideyoshi. It is popular for its beaches, old temples and orange groves. Sandy Sunset Beach on the west coast is, as its name suggests, a good spot to be at the end of the day.

Before then, however, be sure to visit the amazing temple, Kosanji, in Setoda, the main port. It's the brainchild of one man, Kanemoto Kozo, who made a fortune out of manufacturing steel pipes in the 1920s and then decided to become a priest. The temple is dedicated to his mother, who is worshipped as an incarnation of Kannon, the Goddess of Mercy. You can see a sculpture of her as the goddess in the Choseikaku, a villa Kozo built for her in 1927. Next to it is a five-storey pagoda based on Muroji at Nara, while the rest of the complex is made up of copies of famous temples from around Japan. Not far from the main temple building, take a look inside the Senbutsudo, a cave packed with a thousand Buddhas.

Islands of all shapes and sizes are dotted around the Inland Sea.

Omi-shima

This was another important base for medieval pirates. A little way beyond the island's port of Miyaura, the Oyamazumi-jinja is a shrine dedicated to the patron god of sailors, where the pirates worshipped before setting off for battle. It's one of the oldest shrines in Japan, and for centuries received suits of samurai armour and swords as votive offerings, which means that today the Treasure Hall has the most impressive collection of samurai hardware in the country.

The Kaiji Museum next door also has its origins in the sea, and contains a collection of objects connected to marine biology. Here you'll perhaps be surprised to discover that Emperor Hirohito was a keen marine biologist. The museum has his specially built research boat on display, as well as a range of pickled ocean creatures and stuffed sea birds.

The classic inferno of Io volcano in Akan National Park.

Hokkaido

Stretching northwards towards Siberia, Hokkaido was the domain of the Ainu, the aboriginal people who had once inhabited all of Japan's main islands. After the 1860s, Japanese expansion saw Ainu language and culture effectively marginalized, though there has been a noticeable revival of late among the remaining Ainu population.

By Japanese standards, this large, mountainous island is a sparsely populated expanse of wide-open spaces. With its warm, typhoon-free summers and long, cold winters it's great for outdoor activities such as hiking, skiing and white water rafting

Hakodate

Located by the Tsugaru Strait, which divides Hokkaido from Honshu, Hakodate was controlled by the Ainu till the 18th century, when it became a base for the Japanese fishing industry. Part of Japan's eagerness to take over the town was due to nervousness over the number of Russian ships that used the port, and Hakodate still has reminders of its Russian connection, including a fine Russian Orthodox church of 1859. It is in Motomachi, a charming district of cobblestone streets and 19th-century buildings sandwiched between the harbour and Mt Hakodate.

North of the church, the Old British Consulate is an atmospheric place to stop for tea. From a short distance south of the church, you can take a cable car to the top of Mt Hakodate (334 m) for superb views, especially at night.

A walk towards the harbour brings you to the Museum of Northern Peoples, an essential place to visit for those interested in the history and culture of Hokkaido's original Ainu population. West of here on a hill overlooking the port is the fascinating Foreigners' Cemetery. Hakodate was, along with Kobe and Yokohama, one of the few towns open to Westerners in the 19th century and the cemetery contains the graves of Russians, French, British, Chinese and American citizens, including two sailors from Commodore Perry's epoch-making mission to Japan in 1854.

Close to the main railway station, the vibrant Asa-ichi morning market shouldn't be missed. Get there before 8 a.m. if possible to witness the extravaganza of the market's fresh fish stalls: Hokkaido is one of Japan's biggest sources of fish, including snow crab, squid and sea urchin.

Goryo-kaku

From Hakodate's fish market you can catch a tram to this unusual star-shaped fortress, 5 km east of the city centre. Dating from the mid-19th century, it was Japan's first castle built in the western style. Now it is Hakodate's prime *sakura*-viewing location, with its 4000 cherry trees blossoming in late April or early May.

Sapporo

Hokkaido's economic and political centre came to the world's attention in 1972 when it hosted the Winter Olympics, though it's probably just as well known these days for being the home of Sapporo beer. It was a small Ainu village until 1821, when a Japanese trading post was established here. After the Meiji Restoration in 1868 it was made the island's capital and grew rapidly in size and importance. This city of almost 2 million inhabitants has been described as "Tokyo North", and certainly its glittering lights and vast scale have more in common with the great metropolis to the south than the vast wilderness of Hokkaido.

The modern city's construction began in 1871 in a grid design, based on the advice of American engineers. At its heart is the famous landmark Clock Tower, not far from Odori Station. A fairly unprepossessing building of 1878, this contains a small local history museum. Just south of here, Odori Park is a popular flower-adorned thoroughfare and the centrepiece of the Yuki Matsuri snow festival in February and the Sapporo Beer Festival from mid-July to Mid-August. At the eastern end, the 90-m TV Tower —similar in appearance to the

Mighty Tunnel? The Seikan Tunnel connecting Honshu and Hokkaido, is, at 53.85 km, the longest railway tunnel in the world. It runs beneath the Tsugaru Straits, a dangerous stretch of water in bad weather where, in 1954, more than 1,400 ferry passengers died when their ship went down in a typhoon. The next year, Japan Railways began planning an underwater alternative, though the Seikan wasn't completed until 1988 at a cost of $3.6 billion. Criticism of the cost was boosted by the fact that in the intervening years the tunnel seemed to have become superannuated due to the onset of cheap air travel. And yet, with a new, ecologically minded generation of travellers and the advent of carbon offsets aimed at air transport, perhaps its day is still to come. JR certainly believe so—their new Shinkansen-quality line is due to open in 2015. What's more, visitors to Hakodate interested in finding out more can arrange to go on a tour of the tunnel via the city's JR reservation centre.

one in Tokyo—has excellent 360° views from the top. Make your way back along Odori Park and turn right. Three blocks to the north is the Hokudai Shokubutsuen, a fine botanical garden with more than 4000 plant varieties.

Not far from the city centre are good opportunities to find out more about the things that really put Sapporo on the map. Around a kilometre to the east, the Sapporo Beer Garden and Museum is located in the original Sapporo Brewery, built in 1876 as the first brewery in Japan. There's a 50-minute tour covering the history of beer in Japan and concluding with a free tasting.

The Sapporo Winter Sports Museum, west of the city centre, focuses on winter sports in general, though its best exhibits are connected to the 1972 Winter Olympics, including the 101-m slope of the ski jump. Climb to the top for the chance to do a simulated jump of your own.

Jozankei Onsen
This is one of Japan's most famous spa resorts, 35 km southwest of Sapporo. It has good hotels and lots of steaming hot water in which to recuperate after a hard day's sightseeing.

Shikotsu-Toya National Park
Stretching across a large area around 80 km south of Sapporo, the national park is an area of magnificent scenery and seething volcanic activity. Lake Toya, at the western extremity of the park, is a stunning circular caldera lake with four wooded islands. Toyako Onsen is a busy spa resort on the southwestern shore. Nearby, the Showa Shin-zan volcano suddenly appeared in 1943 and grew to 400 m over the next two years. It regularly belches out smoke, as does the neighbouring Usu-zan, which erupted as recently as 2000. You can find out more about the region's volcanoes at the Abuta Volcano Science Museum near the bus station in Toyako Onsen.

Noboribetsu
Hokkaido's most popular *onsen* is 25 km away, in a delightful mountainside setting with several different types of hot spring, and where the water is heated by a volcanic inferno.

Around Hokkaido
Beyond the main cities, Hokkaido is a vast, empty terrain boasting a number of spectacular national parks, windswept capes and open wetlands. Here, you can spend days striking out on your own with just the magnificent wildlife and the mountains for company. It is without doubt a far cry from the usual image of crowded, urban Japan.

Cape Erimo

On a remote thumb of land jutting southwards into the Pacific Ocean, Erimo-misaki is as famous for the power of the wind as the beauty of the scenery. Until recently the hills around the cape were bare, the black pine trees that once covered them having been cut down in the years of Japanese industrialization following the Meiji Period. The ecological effects of this threatened to ruin the local kelp farmers' ancient industry, but a vigorous programme of replanting means that these days visitors will be greeted by a pine forest and a flourishing kelp-farming community.

The farmers' boats can easily be seen off the coast here, where they trawl the kelp beds. Look out too for the distinctive white-spotted Kuril seals that come up onto the rocks on the shore, a sight much beloved of Japanese tourists. At the tip of the cape you'll be treated to a photogenic lighthouse—and the full force of the wind. So famous is this that there's a wind museum here, too. The Kaze-no-Yakata deals with all aspects of the elements, but the liveliest part is a tunnel in which you can experience what it's like to be in a gale-force wind.

Kushiro Shitsugen National Park

Located around 150 km to the east, the park is in effect a gigantic marsh. As such, it attracts an enormous array of wildlife, though is best known for its colony of red-crested cranes *(tan-cho-zuru)*. These elegant birds, with their famously balletic mating dance, are emblematic of Japan, though this didn't prevent them from almost becoming extinct. There are now hundreds of pairs and they can easily be seen here in winter and early spring. Dedicated birdwatchers will want to bring binoculars to enjoy the show to the full.

Getting around the 269 sq km of the park's wetlands isn't always easy, so it's probably a good idea to take advantage of the scenic train that chugs along the edge of the marsh. Ride on it at night and there's an even better chance of spotting the wildlife going about their business.

Akan National Park

Just 50 km north from Kushiro, this magnificent 900-sq-km park is crammed with natural wonders, including a couple of active volcanoes, three major caldera lakes and large tracts of primeval forest. The park is great for hiking trips, though it might be a good idea to rent a car in order to get to the more remote starting points.

Some of the most picturesque spots are around the lakes. Mashu-ko, in the eastern part of the park, is acclaimed for its

A clean break. Japan has an extraordinary number of thermal bath possibilities, but an established etiquette should be observed at all of them. Taking a bath here is a communal affair, a chance to unwind with friends of the same sex. You would shock and offend the fastidious Japanese if you simply disrobed, entered the tub and sat down. Before you get into the bath you must wash yourself clean — and, by scooping water over yourself from the *onsen*, you will not only gradually acclimatize to its temperature but will also be seen to be washing by the other bathers. Generally, taps, pails and soap are on hand near the bath for these preliminaries. The actual bath water, which should preferably be very hot indeed, is shared by all. Bathing costumes aren't worn — most *onsen* provide a small towel with which to wash yourself and protect your modesty. The minerals take 6 hours to be absorbed by the skin, so don't rinse afterwards in anything other than the spring water. Afterwards, take a non-alcoholic drink and relax before embarking on a more energetic programme.

beauty, set within sheer walls of rock and with startlingly clear water. Kushiro-ko, 15 km to the west, is the largest of the park's lakes. It's a perfect spot for swimming and other water sports as well as relaxing in the *onsen*, where the water and sand are both heated courtesy of volcanic power. On this same subject, the Io-zan volcano, located between the two lakes, is a classic "hell", where hot steam belches out from vents in the mountainside, sulphurous mud oozes from the ground, and eggs can be boiled in natural pools. Needless to say, this all adds up to making this one of the region's most popular resorts.

Akan-ko, to the southwest, is surrounded by thick pine forests and dominated by two volcanoes, including the active Me-Akan-dake. Curiously, it's most famous among Japanese visitors for the small balls of duckweed found in the lake itself. Known locally as *marimo*, this extremely rare species exerts a fascination way beyond its size, taking up to 200 years to form, bobbing up to the surface after absorbing oxygen from the water, then releasing the gas and sinking again. During the October *marimo* festival, stray duckweed balls are reintroduced into the lake.

For a close-up view of some *marimo*, check out the Eco Museum Centre in Akan Kohan, a spa town at the southern tip of the lake which has a sizeable Ainu settlement at its edge. The Ainu Kotan Village has thatched houses, Ainu shops and performances of traditional Ainu dance six times a day in summer. Further information about the Ainu can be found at the Akan Forest and Lake Culture Museum.

Shiretoko National Park

Occupying a sharp horn of land on the northeastern coast of Hokkaido, bounded by the Sea of Okhotsk on one side and looking across to the disputed Russian-owned Kuril Islands on the other, the Shiretoko National Park more than merits its place in Ainu mythology as the end of the world. The landscape here can be treacherous for the unwary and inexperienced, with paths disappearing into sheer cliff faces, formidably rough terrain, and the possibility of coming face to face with wild bears.

For the determined hiker, the rewards are immense. There's probably no part of Japan less affected by human activity, and encountering the peninsula's pristine waterfalls, forests and mountains, it's easy to feel like you're the first traveller ever to reach here. Before setting out on any adventure into the park, be sure to visit the Shiretoko Nature Centre, at the entrance to the western side, which has lots of handy information about what to expect once you get onto the peninsula.

You can also come forearmed with maps and other useful nuggets of information if you've begun your journey from Shari, a small town that acts as something of a gateway to Shiretoko. Before leaving, though, take the time to see the Koshimizu Gensei Kaen, a long stretch of coastline heading away from the town that sports a vast number of different species of wildflowers that bloom spectacularly each summer.

Wakkanai

This is the most northerly of Japan's mainland cities, and from the Centennial Memorial Tower, on a hilltop in Wakkanai-koen close to the centre of town, the Russian island of Sakhalin can be seen on a clear day. The park also has a memorial to the dogs that pulled the sleds on Japan's first polar expedition. Wakkanai is where the National Dogsled tournament is held each February. Weather-wise, this feels as much Siberia as Japan.

Heading eastwards along the coast you'll notice the kelp-drying yards—Wakkanai is first and foremost a kelp-farming town. A short distance beyond these is Cape Noshappu, a popular picnic and sunset-watching spot. And, a further 30 km away is Cape Soya, Japan's northernmost point.

Rishiri-Rebun-Sarobetsu National Park

Reached from Wakkanai by ferry or plane, the National Park is made up mainly of two islands, Rishiri and Rebun.

Circular Rishiri is the closest to the mainland and a magnet for hikers in the summer months. What attracts them is the 1,721-m Rishiri-zan, a superb conical volcano rising from the centre of the island in a striking northern echo of Mt Fuji. There are several trails leading to the top, with the most accessible leaving from Oshidomari and Kutsugata. The hike to the top takes around 5 hours. Bear in mind that it's cold there at all times of the year. The best way to recover from the ascent is to stop at the Rishiri-fuji Onsen near the start of the Oshidomari trail, where you can get great views of the mountain along with a hot soak.

For the Ainu, Shiretoko is the end of the world. | Wildlife display for photo-shoot at Akan Eco Museum.

Rebun-to, an elongated island around 10 km north of Rishiri, has a less demanding mountain. A trip to the top of the 490-m Rebun-dake and back takes under 4 hours. It offers fine views of the island and the chance to see some of the hundreds of species of wildflower that grow on Rebun-to. There are plenty of other fine hiking trails that centre on the island's wildflowers, notably one starting from close to the southern port of Kafuka and one round the northern Cape Sukoton.

Ishite-ji, Stone Hand Temple, is 51st of the 88 temples on the Shikoku pilgrimage route.

Shikoku

Shikoku is the smallest of Japan's four main islands and one of the country's best-kept tourist secrets, remaining off the beaten track even for most Japanese visitors. The island's name, pronounced in two syllables, *shko-koo*, means quite simply "four provinces"—Kagawa and Tokushima to the east, Ehime to the northwest along the Inland Sea and Kochi to the south, facing the Pacific Ocean. Divided by a central mountain range running from east to west, Shikoku has two distinct climates—bright and sunny to the north of the mountains and much warmer, but rainier, to the south.

Matsuyama

In the western Ehime Province, Shikoku's largest city, with a population of more than 450,000, enjoys an unhurried pace and a reputation from the past as a city of art and culture. It also has Shikoku's finest castle and an acclaimed *onsen* to enjoy.

Matsuyama Castle

Built in 1602–03, Matsuyama Castle was struck by lightning and burnt down in the 18th century; it was not rebuilt until the 1850s, making the current late Edo-era fortress not only one of the best-preserved but also most recent of Japan's "original" castles. It was the stronghold of the Matsudaira clan, loyal lieutenants of the Tokugawa shoguns, for whom they planted cedar forests on the mainland reminiscent of the splendid trees surrounding their castle here. The trees blanket the castle's hill as part of Shiroyama Park. Unlike most castles in Japan, you can reach this one via a cable car.

Dogo Spa

Just 2 km from the city centre, this renowned old public bathhouse is a good place to unwind in the Japanese manner. It was the model for the one in Miyazaki's film *Spirited Away*. The alkaline waters of the crystal-clear hot springs are said to soothe nerves, lungs and stomach upsets.

The springtime cherry blossoms in the nearby Dogo Park will also lift the spirits.

Zentsuji

As the birthplace in 774 of the great Buddhist priest Kobo Daishi, this temple is one of the most hallowed shrines in Japan. Founded in 813, it was rebuilt in the 17th century, with a five-storey pagoda added in 1882. In the treasure house at the rear of the main worship-hall are works by the man revered for introducing the Shingon "True Word" sect to Japan from China in 804. Zentsuji is the sect's headquarters and 75th in the pilgrims' itinerary around the island's 88 temples.

Kotohiragu

Some 5 km south of Zentsuji and known more informally as the Kompira-san, this is an equally revered Shinto shrine, its deity being the protector of travellers and sailors. Stone steps lead up the 521-m Mt Zozu to the *daimon* (entrance gate) set in a grove of cherry trees. The lovely natural setting is characteristic of a Shinto shrine's location: the richly decorated buildings—tea hall and parlour as well as worship-hall and sacred music hall—loom in a dense forest of pine, cedar and camphor trees.

Note that the climb up to the main shrine is fairly strenuous, though you can be carried up in a palanquin—at a price.

Takamatsu

A short distance east of these temples, Shikoku's main gateway for air and sea traffic from Honshu was founded in the 16th century by Toyotomi Hideyoshi as a fortress town and served to protect both the Kagawa region and the pirate-packed Inland Sea. These days its main attraction is the more peaceful Ritsurin Park.

Ritsurin Park

A couple of kilometres back from the harbour, this is a masterful combination of classical Japanese garden architecture with the simple pleasures of a public park. Its 76 ha are beautifully landscaped with strangely shaped rocks and gnarled pine trees among the ponds, waterways and hillocks. Visit the Museum of Folk Art or take tea presented in a ceremony of grace and simplicity at the Kiku-getsu-tei pavilion, whose garden of rock and white gravel is a fine example of Zen design.

Yashima

Around 5 km east of the centre, the Yashima Plateau has spectacular views of the Inland Sea and Shikoku coastline. It was here, in 1182, that the boy emperor Antoku and his Taira clan protectors were defeated by the Minamoto clan, leading to the establishment of the Shogunate at Kamakura. Yashimaji—84th in the 88-temple pilgrimage—houses a museum containing relics from the battles on land and sea.

Naruto

From the Naruto Straits at the eastern tip of the island, you can witness the natural phenomenon of violent whirlpools. These are created by water rushing at rapid speed into and out of the Inland Sea, in the narrow channel between Awaji-shima and Shikoku, during high and low tides.

Kochi

The only big town on Shikoku's Pacific coast, with a population of

320,000, is an agricultural centre and a fishing port specializing in bonito. As such it's a good place for food markets, though the general Sunday market on the palm-lined road up to the castle is excellent and shouldn't be missed.

Kochi Castle
This is another early 17th-century castle destroyed by fire and later rebuilt. The five-storey keep—all that remains of the original fortress—dates from 1753 and has superb views over the city and Urado Bay. The *kaitokukan*, or living quarters, of the feudal lords who inhabited the castle is open to the public.

Godaisan Park
Take the cable car to the lovely Godaisan Park on a hill southeast of town, where there are fine panoramas over the city. Inside the park is Chikurinji temple, founded in 724 and number 32 on the 88-temple pilgrimage. The park boasts a botanical garden with thousands of tropical plants.

Ryugado Cave
Some 20 km to the east, the cave was discovered in 1931 when archaeologists unearthed traces of the island's earliest inhabitants. They found *yayoi* (wheel-made) clay dishes dating back to the last centuries before the Christian era. With its limestone stalagmites and stalactites, the cavern winds underground for some 4 km. One of its largest chambers has a cupola-like ceiling 30 m high.

Agnès Curchod

Pilgrimage. The Buddhist priest Kukai (posthumously named Kobo Daishi) was born in Zentsuji in 774. Credited with inventing the *hiragana* syllabary that incorporated Chinese characters into Japanese writing, he also founded the Shingon (True Word) sect, based on the belief that enlightenment can be achieved in this life. Many of the temples he established are in Shikoku, and in 835, the last year of his life, he set off on a pilgrimage around 88 of the island's temples, covering a distance of some 1,450 km. It has been Japan's most famous pilgrimage ever since and is undertaken each year by pilgrims clad in white tunics, mittens and leggings. Whereas Kukai travelled on foot, however, most of the pilgrims these days follow the route by bus.

A cloud of steam rises from the the waters of Umi Jigoku—Ocean Hell, at Beppu.

Rainer Hackenberg

Kyushu

With its sunny climate, friendly population and easy-going way of life, the southernmost of Japan's four main islands can feel positively Mediterranean. Its proximity to the Asian mainland, with the Korean peninsula just across the Japan Sea, has also made it more open to foreign influences than the rest of the country. This was the channel for Chinese and Korean cultural innovations that have coloured Japanese civilization over the centuries, while the port city of Nagasaki was where the first Westerners set foot in Japan in the mid-16th century. Kyushu itself is largely rural and mountainous, with considerable volcanic activity, from towering Mt Aso, one of the world's largest active volcanoes, to the boiling mud pots of Beppu. To relax, however, there are several beach resorts where you can bury yourself up to the neck in soothing, warm volcanic sands.

Beppu

The east-coast spa town is probably the most successful of all Ja-pan's resorts, its permanent population of about 150,000 boosted by an estimated 13 million visitors each year. They come for the reviving properties of the hot springs and the entertainment value of the "Hells", pools of boiling water that make the city notoriously steamy and sulphurous.

Hot springs

In and around Beppu are eight hot springs, each with different natural chemical properties said to cure every ailment under the sun. Among the star attractions are the Hotta Hot Springs, outdoor baths in ponds scenically situated among the rocks of a waterfall at the Shibaseki spring; the mud bath at Kannawa and hot sands bath at Takegawara, where there is also a wonderful old-fashioned public bath.

Hell pools

Not to be missed is a Hell Ponds tour around Kannawa. A hundred crocodiles snooze in the hot waters of Devil's Mountain Hell *(Oniyama Jigoku)*. Monk's Hell *(Bozu Jigoku)* is a huge bubbling mud pond concealing in its depths a Buddhist temple buried 500 years ago by an earthquake. The steaming pond of Blood Pool Hell *(Chinoike Jigoku)* has been turned blood-red by its iron oxide. You can boil eggs in baskets in the seething waters of Ocean Hell *(Umi Jigoku)*.

Beyond Beppu

To the west, the rustic farmhouses of the charming country village of Yufuin make it a haven of old-fashioned peace after the boisterous modernity of the resort. You may find some delicious honey or nicely crafted bamboo-ware.

Part of the Kuju mountain range southwest of Beppu, Kuju Plateau offers many delightful possibilities for walks across meadows with grazing horses and cattle.

Mount Aso National Park

The great mountain Takadake, 1,585 m at its highest point, offers a sweeping panorama of the five volcanic craters that make up the Aso caldera. The site is enormous, with the outer crater measuring almost 130 km in circumference. Only one volcano, Nakadake (1,506 m), is still active. From the rim you can peer down into the bleak wilderness of its crater, which occasionally puffs out sulphurous smoke. There are shelters here in case of sudden eruptions, put in place after 12 visitors were killed in 1958.

The park's mountain slopes and plateaux present a landscape of brilliant emerald-green mounds carpeted with bright pink azaleas. Aso Volcanic Museum vividly documents earthquakes and eruptions with audio-visual special effects and film from inside Nakadake.

Nagasaki

When the first Europeans—Portuguese traders—arrived in 1542, Nagasaki, in the northwest of Kyushu, was little more than a fishing village. Christian missionaries followed soon after and claimed many converts, including the first Christian feudal lord Omura Sumitada. Fearing the spread of the religion, the Tokugawa shogunate expelled the Portuguese in 1639, though it permitted Dutch traders to inhabit a small island in Nagasaki harbour—the only Japanese contact with the West for 220 years. The city was opened to foreigners again from 1859, and it was this period that inspired the setting for Puccini's opera *Madame Butterfly*. In 1945 Nagasaki was the target of the second Atomic Bomb attack, which destroyed much of the city in a matter of seconds. Its recovery was miraculous, and the city is now devoted to the abolition of nuclear weapons. Today, Nagasaki is a thriving industrial centre of 450,000 people, including a substantial Chinese community. Along with all the attractions of modern Japan are several reminders of its fascinating past.

The setting is magnificent: ideally situated in an amphitheatre of green hills next to a deep bay and enclosed by a peninsula, it is one of world's great natural harbours. The city centre offers numerous scenic panoramas, while most of the sights themselves are only a short distance back from the water's edge.

Note that Nagasaki is very hilly, so be prepared for some

fairly demanding walks. Around Glover Gardens, however, there are lifts and escalators to help you up.

Around Central Station

Just north of the station is the site where European and Japanese Christians were crucified in 1597 during the reign of Hideyoshi Toyotomi. A cross-shaped Martyrs' Memorial is dedicated to them, with a relief of the 26 martyrs (the youngest of whom was 12 years old) carved on the outer wall, and a small museum of Christian relics.

Head north from here and then turn left, crossing the Urakami River, which flows into the harbour. Nearby is a cable car that takes you to the summit of Mt Inasa, 332 m high. It commands a fantastic view of the city and harbour from a lush setting inhabited by deer and other wildlife.

Shofukuji, a temple 200 m east of the Central Station, dates from the 18th century and has fine gardens with good views of the port. Further on, a flight of 73 stone steps leads up to the Suwa Shrine, built in 1555 and remarkable for its huge bronze *torii*, a graceful, curved gateway reputedly the highest in Japan. The shrine comes alive in October as the focus for the Kunchi Matsuri festival, with plenty of dragon dancing and drumming.

Chinese temples

Down the hill towards the bay is a colony of Chinese-built Buddhist temples; they were intended to counteract the influence of Christianity in the 17th century. In its pleasant palm-tree setting, Kofukuji (1629) was the first Obaku Zen temple to be built in Japan. Notice the Chinese-mandarin moustaches on statues of the temple's abbots. Over the Nakajima river, a double-arched bridge, Meganebashi, was built by Kofukuji's first abbot in 1634.

Most beautiful of the city's temples is Sofukuji. Also known as the Temple of Nanking, it was founded in 1635 and is a fine example of late Ming architecture, set amid tall trees and lovely landscaping. The distinctive, squat entrance arch is one of the most recognizable images of Nagasaki; the main hall was built in China and transported here in 1646.

Dejima

The fan-shaped artificial island in Nagasaki Harbour on which Dutch traders lived from 1641 to 1854 has been overtaken by land reclamation, but it is now undergoing an impressive restoration process and there are even plans to make it an island once again. Almost all the original buildings, have been reconstructed; many are furnished with period décor and are open to the public. A

museum shows fascinating pictures of Dejima in the early days and has displays covering the history of the Dutch in Nagasaki.

Around Glover Gardens

South of the port terminal is the cobbled street of Oranda-zaka (Hollander Slope), with reconstructions of redbrick and clapboard houses of Western traders who came here after 1859.

British traders left their mark with their 19th-century houses at Glover Gardens, set on a hillside about a kilometre west of Hollander Slope. You can take an escalator or an elevator up the hill to peruse the massive Victorian furniture and bric-a-brac. A sailors' lodging house has been converted into a little naval museum with models of old Chinese junks and new Japanese oil tankers, while the picturesque Jiyu-tei teahouse, moved here from the centre, was the first Western-style restaurant in Japan.

The gardens' centrepiece is Glover House, home of Scottish merchant Thomas Blake Glover, who moved to Nagasaki at the age of 21 and became a leading

The volcanic slopes of Mt Aso National Park cloaked in a tapestry of autumn colours. | Kagoshima is blessed with fertile soil thanks to the close presence of Mt Sakurajima.

figure in the city's industrial development. More romantically, it is reputed to be the place in which Madame Butterfly fell in love with Pinkerton, or so Puccini imagined it. A statue of Japanese opera singer Tamaki Miura in the role of Cho-Cho San can be found just uphill from the house.

Urakami

This residential quarter around 2.5 km north of Nagasaki city centre was wiped out by the atom bomb dropped on August 9, 1945 —a mistake caused by heavy fog concealing the original target, the Mitsubishi steel works. The area has several memorials of that terrible event.

Atomic Bomb Museum

Any visit to the museum, which opened in 1996, is a powerful and haunting experience. The exhibits begin with a clock that stopped at 11.02 a.m., the instant when 70,000 people were killed, and meticulously document scenes of Nagasaki before and after the bombing. Some of the photos and testimonies of the victims are very disturbing indeed. Outside the main rooms there are video displays attempting to place the bombing in the wider context of Japan's involvement in the war, with a brief mention of Pearl Harbour. A special section is devoted to nuclear proliferation over the decades since the bomb was dropped and the call for a future without nuclear weapons.

Hypocentre Park

Just below the museum, the park has a black marble column marking the exact spot above which the atom bomb detonated. Next to it is a fragment of Urakami Cathedral, which had been the largest church in Asia till that moment. This has since been rebuilt in its original location around 600 m east of the park.

Peace Park

North of the Atomic Bomb Museum is this small Peace Park, with Kitamuro Seibo's dramatic memorial statue in bronze, 9.5-m-high, personifying Peace. The park is on the site of Urakami Prison, the closest public building to the blast. All 134 of the workers and inmates died instantly.

Kagoshima

With its warm, southern climate, bayside location and adjacent active volcano, Kagoshima merits its nickname of Naples of the East. Mt Sakurajima, the volcano in question, may not be able to compete with Fuji for grace and prestige, but its outpourings of smoke couldn't be more dramatic. Besides the medicinal hot springs in and around the town, this volcanic activity also works agricultural miracles on the soil. It produces everything from football-size radishes to miniature mandarin oranges, named *satsuma* after the region, while the mellow climate is responsible for a profusion of palm trees and lush floral displays.

The pleasant city of 400,000 inhabitants was the feudal seat of the Shimazu clan for nearly 800 years from the 12th century till the Meiji Restoration, when Takamori Saigo, the last bastion of samurai feudalism, was defeated by the emperor's troops. Today, its charms are largely of the outdoor variety, walking around a Shimazu-era garden or strolling through its relaxed, sunny streets. See it all, and the volcano across the bay, from a transparent gondola on the ferris wheel of Amu Plaza shopping centre next to the railway station.

Iso Gardens

This big park on the edge of the Isoyama Mountains, 1.5 km north of the city centre, was originally the estate of the Shimazu princes who ruled Kagoshima for centuries. It contains recreation grounds, a small museum, a restaurant and a souvenir shop. But it's the formal Japanese garden that really captivates. Laid out in the 17th century, it demonstrates the refined aesthetic sensibility within Japanese horticulture, where the utmost care has gone into finding the ideal position for every tree, shrub, flower and stone, and using the ponds, the sky and the mountains to frame them.

Foreigners' Residence

On the way back to town, you'll glimpse a most un-Japanese work of architecture: the vaguely Victorian-style Foreigners' Residence, Ijinkan, built to accommodate the British technical experts who helped establish the country's first fully-fledged textile industry. As ever, the Japanese wanted the expatriates to feel at home, hence this attempt to create comfortable European-style quarters.

Shiroyama Park

For a good view of the city of Kagoshima and the volcano, the place to go is Shiroyama Park, in the hills just west of the town centre, planted with subtropical trees and lush ferns. A museum in the park is devoted to the life and battles of local hero Takamori Saigo, last great champion of the samurai. After initially supporting the Meiji Restoration he turned against its reforming intention to abolish the samurai class. He was defeated in 1877 and joined his fellow warriors in *seppuku*, or ritual suicide.

Monuments

Among the city's many statues and monuments, Westerners will note the bronze bust of the Jesuit Francis Xavier, patron saint of Catholic missionaries who landed in Kagoshima in 1549. The commemorative ensemble includes stones from the first Christian church built in Kagoshima, in the 16th century.

The Satsuma-no-Gunzo Monument features the statues of 17 young men sent from Kagoshima to England in 1865 to study technology. The revolutionary push to modernization encouraged by the Shimazu family is emphasized here by the students' formal European attire.

Sakurajima

Ferryboats shuttle between central Kagoshima and the volcanic peninsula of Sakurajima. Its foothills are carpeted with greenery; higher up the scenery is black and bleak. Until the 20th century the volcano occupied an island in Kagoshima Bay. Now it forms a peninsula, for the lava that raged down the hillside in the momentous eruption of 1914 solidified into a broad, firm isthmus. The volcano's circumference is now about 52 km, one-third bigger than before the eruption.

As for the spectacle at the summit, altitude 1,117 m, the scene changes from minute to minute depending on the weather and winds—and the mood of the volcano within. At times, it asserts itself with spectacular blasts of black smoke, and the volcanic dust settles almost imperceptibly over Kagoshima, most noticeably after rain.

Assuming Sakurajima doesn't blow its top on the day you visit, you should take a tour through the lava fields. Local sightseeing buses offer varied itineraries lasting 1 to 2.5 hours, revealing the way the 12,000 inhabitants of the sooty slopes have carved out a successful agricultural life.

At Furusato, on the peninsula's south coast, there is a complex of hot springs resort hotels.

Ibusuki

This major resort town is just an hour's ride by express train from Kagoshima. Its therapeutic hot springs pour forth 120,000 tons of steaming water per day. But what's special in Ibusuki is the natural "sauna baths". All year round, enthusiasts bury themselves up to their chins in the hot volcanic sand of the beach—claimed to cure all kinds of ills. The deeper you dig, the hotter it gets.

On the edge of town, a huge resort hotel has its own hot springs, sauna, swimming pool, gardens and entertainment programmes.

Okinawa

Okinawa is the largest of the Ryukyu Islands, 500 km southwest of Kyushu. For centuries they were a semi-autonomous kingdom, as much influenced by China as Japan. Indeed, it was a 17th-century Chinese ban on the carrying of weapons by peasants that led to the development here of the unarmed combat technique of karate. During the Meiji period, Okinawa became a Japanese prefecture; the next century it was the scene of one of the bloodiest battles of World War II.

In April 1945, US troops staged an amphibious landing on Iwo Jima and over the next three months 12,000 American soldiers were killed, while the Japanese lost 100,000 soldiers and perhaps as many civilians. It was the ferocity of the resistance here—in what was considered to be part of the Japanese homeland—that led in large part to the decision to drop atomic bombs on Hiroshima and Nagasaki. The US has maintained a large military presence on the island since the war.

Okinawa has a year-round subtropical climate and is surrounded by coral reefs and warm tropical

A lone fisherman lost in the blue seas of Okinawa. | The double-door Gate of Courtesy leading into Shuri Castle was rebuilt in 1958.

waters that are popular with scuba divers and snorkellers. Its interior is mainly rural and agricultural, but Okinawa's laid-back resorts and sandy beaches also make it a playground for Japanese visitors from the mainland in search of stress-free sunshine.

Naha
The island's main city was also capital of the Ryukyu kingdom, which lasted from 1429 to 1879. It was almost completely levelled in 1945, so most of what you see today is post-war reconstruction.

The town centre has some interesting features: the principal street, Kokusai-dori, is filled with shops and restaurants, while to the east of it, Heiwa-dori is a lively market area of covered passageways and alleys. You can also check out the nearby Tsuboya pottery area, with several traditional potteries still in action.

Not far from Tomari port, look out for the Commodore Perry Memorial: Perry, whose well-armed ships forced Japan to open up to world trade in 1853, used Okinawa as his base.

Shuri
Just over a kilometre east of the town centre, the Shuri district was the site of the Ryukyu capital. The royal castle was destroyed in the war, but has been subsequently restored: most striking of all is the classic Okinawan-style Shurei-no-mon (Gate of Courtesy). A reconstruction of 1958, it has become totemic of a distinctive Okinawan culture.

Northern Okinawa
Okinawa becomes significantly less developed the further north you go. The Motobu Peninsula on the northwest coast has superb beaches and crystal-clear seawater and is a magnet for scuba divers. From here, it's worth heading all the way up to the spectacular scenery of the remote Cape Hedo, the northernmost point on Okinawa.

World War II Battlefields
The Battle of Okinawa took place predominantly in the south of the island. Around 5 km south of Naha is the Underground Naval Headquarters, a warren of tunnels and corridors where 4000 Japanese servicemen committed suicide as the battle came to its end. Another 10 km to the south, near the coast, the Memorial Peace Park contains an excellent museum detailing the horrors of the three-month battle and its effects on the island's indigenous population. There are numerous memorials in the park; the biggest is the Cornerstone of Peace, inscribed with the names of all the dead, Japanese, American and Okinawan.

CULTURAL NOTES

Ainu

There's still considerable debate about where the Ainu came from. Now numbering just 24,000, they are found only in Hokkaido, though they once occupied the whole country. Physically different from the Japanese—they have brunette hair and "round" eyes, and the men can grow long beards—they might, according to one theory, be descended from an early Caucasian people who came across northern Asia. A more recent idea, however, is that they are the last remaining descendants of the Jomon, the people who inhabited Japan before the Yayoi (ancestors of the modern Japanese) arrived in 400 BC. In this sense they are the original natives of Japan, a status officially recognized by the Japanese government in 1997.

Akira Kurosawa

Born the son of a gym teacher in Tokyo, Kurosawa (1910–98) later went to art school and became an award-winning artist, but abandoned painting for cinema in the mid-1930s. He worked as an assistant director to the wartime filmmaker Kajiro Yamamoto before progressing to the director's chair in 1943. One of his first movies, a version of a *kabuki* play called *They Who Step on the Tiger's Tail*, was banned in 1945 by the American occupiers, who forbade all films dealing with Japan's feudal past.

Kurosawa's big breakthrough came in 1951 with the pioneering *Rashomon*. Set in 12th-century Kyoto, the movie filters the events leading up to a murder through four contradictory

The traditional clothing of the Ainu features appliqué.

Rainer Hackenberg

viewpoints. It won the Golden Lion at the Venice Film Festival and gained an audience for Japanese cinema around the world. Kurosawa followed this with *Ikiru* (1952), a profound examination of the spiritual malaise of post-war Japan, and then his masterpiece, *The Seven Samurai* (1954). In this film, the director tells an epic tale of a band of masterless samurai who fight without payment to protect a helpless village from a gang of bandits. Kurosawa juxtaposes the stylized *kabuki* acting of his troupe with action scenes that are dazzlingly fluid and dynamic. His reputation was sealed in the following decades with a series of movies that mixed Western and Japanese forms, culminating in *Ran* (1985), an intensely dramatic samurai version of Shakespeare's *King Lear* set in 16th-century Japan.

Literature

Japan's earliest works of literature were by women (male scribes tended to spend their time copying out Chinese texts), and Shikibu Murasaki's *The Tale of Genji*, written at the start of the 11th century and telling of the machinations of imperial court life, can reasonably claim to be the world's first novel. Since the 19th century, however—and contact with the Western literary tradition—novels by Japanese authors have increasingly sought to convey the strains and stresses on individuals in relation to community, family and self in a changing society.

Though very different in style, works such as *The Makioka Sisters* by Junichiro Tanizaki (1886–1965), *Snow Country* by Nobel laureate Yasunari Kawabata (1899–1972) and *The Setting Sun* by Osamu Dazai (1909–48) all focus on the inroads made into traditional values by the seemingly unstoppable juggernaut of Western-style modernity. A generation younger than these writers, Yukio Mishima (1925–70) is probably the best-known Japanese writer outside Japan. But while his work has often been accused of being "untypical" of Japanese literature, novels like *The Temple of the Golden Pavilion*, which brilliantly enters the mind of the young monk who burnt down Kyoto's Kinkakuji temple in 1950, keep up the interrogation of post-war Japanese society's psychological effects on its individual members.

Contemporary novelists such as Haruki Murakami (b.1949) and Banana Yoshimoto (b.1964) have taken Japanese writing into the

Agnès Curchod

Astro Boy was dreamed up by manga artist Osamu Tezuka.

pop age, where on the surface the country seems to have made the final transformation into an urban, fully industrialized society. Still, key longstanding cultural issues remain at the heart of their work: confrontation with sexual taboos, the issue of conforming to family and social expectations, and the desire for escape into other ways of life. Novels such as Murakami's *Kafka on the Shore* or Yoshimoto's *Kitchen* provide powerful insights into the modern Japanese psyche.

Manga

It sometimes seems that whether commuting, sitting in a café or walking along the street, every schoolchild or businessperson has their head stuck firmly inside a door-step sized comic book. Known as mangas (literally, whimsical drawings), the books are notable for their stylized drawings featuring wide-eyed heroes and heroines, gun-toting robots, and a tendency towards a level of violence and the erotic that might surprise Westerners. The manga craze began after World War II, though some see the bold, colourful artwork as part of a tradition stretching back to Edo woodblock prints. They have now become one of Japan's biggest cultural exports.

Shinto

Most Japanese have a relaxed attitude to religion and don't feel obliged to choose between Shinto and Buddhism—they are as likely to pray at a Buddhist temple as a Shinto shrine. Shinto is the national cult, also known as *kami-no-michi*, "the way of the gods". It is a polytheistic form of nature-worship with shrines in places of great natural beauty such as in forests or on mountaintops. Ritual purification is a prominent feature of the religion, starting by hand and mouth-rinsing when approaching a shrine. Worship itself is surprisingly informal and unsolemn: worshippers clap hands three times to attract the gods' attention, bow respectfully, drop a few coins in the alms-box and whisper a brief prayer before leaving.

Ukiyo-e

Ukiyo-e is the term for the brightly coloured woodblock prints of the 18th and 19th centuries and literally means "pictures of the floating world": the twilight pleasure districts of Edo (Tokyo), Osaka and Kyoto. *Ukiyo-e* originated as art for the common people and was a far cry from the refined, stylized art forms favoured by the aristocracy and the imperial court. Artists like Katsushika Hokusai and Ando Hiroshige gave realistic glimpses of ordinary city life; Kitagawa Utamaro was famous for his sensual portraits of courtesans and prostitutes; and Toshusai Sharaku created 150 remarkable pictures of *kabuki* actors with exaggerated expressions. There was a flourishing trade in erotic *ukiyo-e* prints, while others had a nostalgic vein—some of the best-known prints now are images of rural Japan, such as Hokusai's *The 36 Views of Mount Fuji* and his famous *The Wave*, or Hiroshige's *Fifty-three Stations of the Tokaido*.

These works were printed in great quantities and not thought to merit the status of art or be worthy of collecting. They were often used as packing material for fragile pottery items sent to Europe in tea chests, which is how they came to the attention of European artists later in the 19th century. Their use of colour and innovative sense of perspective had a radical impact on Impressionist and Post-Impressionist artists such as Manet, Degas and Gauguin, as well as Van Gogh who owned several prints and painted many copies of them. In many ways, the woodblock world of old Edo gave birth to modern Europe's best-loved artistic movement.

The Wedded Rocks at Ise represent the Shinto creator gods Izanagi and Izanami.

Rainer Hackenberg

Crocks of *nukazuke*: tangy and crispy vegetable pickles made by fermentation in rice bran, salt and seaweed.

DINING OUT

Japan has one of the world's great cuisines, and an undoubted highlight of any visit is the chance to sample its varied culinary delights. Designed to please the eye as well as the palate, Japanese food is artistically prepared under the most hygienic conditions, with an emphasis on fresh, healthy ingredients and subtle seasonings. Rice, pickles and clear miso soup are standard accompaniments to most meals.

Many of the dishes will be strange to newcomers, but you don't have to read Japanese to survive. Some restaurants have menus with photographs while others display realistic plastic models of their specialities in their windows, marked with the price. If the written menu baffles you, lead the order-taker outside and point to the replica of the dish you fancy. There are often good-value set meals or *teishoku* to be had, especially at lunchtime and even in quite expensive places. Whatever you decide on, it will be even better washed down with sake, Japanese rice wine, or one of the superb lager beers.

To Start With...
Breakfast at a *ryokan* or *minshuku* will likely as not be a traditional Japanese affair of whitebait, pickles, grilled fish, soup and rice. If this isn't your cup of *o-cha* at 8 o'clock in the morning—and many Japanese diners will agree with you on this one—then head for a café. These often have economical set breakfasts *(moningu setto)* that consist of toast, a boiled egg and coffee. In the cities, French-style bakery-cum-cafés and imitation American coffee shops serve pastries, muffins and the like.

Noodles
You'll come across noodle shops in every town, selling bowls of *ramen* (egg noodles), *soba* (buckwheat noodles), generally served cold, and *udon* (wheat flour noodles) in a steaming hot broth. These are especially popular with locals at lunchtime or for a quick snack after work.

Ramen is Chinese in origin. The noodles are served in a bowl of meat broth and come with toppings such as sliced pork and vegetables. Thin, brown *soba* and thicker, white *udon* are home-grown Japanese versions of *ramen* and exist in a wide range of forms such as *sansai-soba/udon* (mountain vegetable), with such things as tiny *nameko* mushrooms, *warabi* (chopped bracken shoots) and *zenmai* (fern shoots); *tempura-soba/udon*, with slices of tempura shrimps; *kitsune-soba/udon*, with pieces of fried tofu; *kamonamban-soba/udon*, with goose or chicken; and *tsukimi-soba/udon*, with an egg cooked on top of the noodles.

Although Westerners are often provided with a soup spoon, it is customary to eat the ingredients with chopsticks and drink the broth directly from the bowl. Loud slurping of the noodles is not considered rude; in fact it is the accepted manner both for cooling and adding to the taste-pleasure.

Other snacks

The local fast-food scene in Japan is a world away from the culture of the Big Mac. *Okonomiyaki* is a cross between an omelette and a pizza, made from egg batter, vegetables, cabbage and meat or fish. Many restaurants will give you the basic ingredients and you make the thing yourself on a hot griddle on your table.

Kushiage means morsels of pork and other meats deep-fried on sticks. With *yakitori*, chunks of chicken, chicken liver or pork are grilled on thin bamboo skewers and served with a barbecue sauce.

Takoyaki (octopus balls) are sold from street stalls: dumplings fried on an iron griddle and enclosing a filling of chopped octopus and vegetables. Pancakes rolled into a cornet shape are sold on every street corner, with sweet or savoury fillings.

Sushi and sashimi

There's a local saying that the best cooking is the least cooking, and that certainly holds true with regard to fish and seafood. They are the mainstays of the Japanese diet, and thanks to the country's long coastline and numerous fishing ports, they are always very fresh and varied, as witnessed by the national passion for eating raw fish, something that relies completely on the quality of the main ingredient.

Sashimi and *sushi*, Japan's most famous culinary exports, both depend on this sense of quality. *Sashimi* is raw fish in its finest state, impeccably fresh, sliced in small bite-size pieces and dipped in soy sauce and a green horseradish known as *wasabi*, with boiled rice served separately, shredded white radish and perhaps a small bowl of broth. It's often served as a first course.

Sushi, on the other hand, are morsels of raw fish, shellfish and roes with vinegared rice and a little *wasabi*. The word *"sushi"* actually refers to the method of preparation, and you'll likely receive such varieties as egg *sushi* in your meal. The best-known type, with fish on top of the rice, is strictly speaking called *nigiri-zushi*, while *sushi* wrapped in seaweed is *maki-sushi*. There are also regional variations to look out for. In Kurashiki in Western Honshu, for example, the local speciality is *mamakari-sushi*, made with sardine.

The cost of each piece of *sushi* is dependent on the particular quality of the fish used, so in a typical set meal you will get a mix of *futsu-nigiri* (standard *sushi*), *jo-nigiri* (higher quality) and *toku-jo nigiri* (the very best quality). The latter will usually mean enjoying such delights as a succulent slice of *ô-toro*, the finest cut of tuna. If you're ordering *sushi* by individual portions it

A selection of colourful specialities. | To make it easier to choose: window display of plastic sushi. | A tasty noodle dish, *hiroshimayaki*. | Pancakes, sweet or savoury, are popular snacks.

can be very expensive, so if prices are not posted, ask first, or the bill may give you a nasty shock. On the other hand, in *kaiten-zushi* (self-service *sushi* restaurants), where the plates circulate on conveyor belts, you pay according to the colour or shape of the plates you choose (you pile the empty plates up on your table). All the extra things you need, such as chopsticks and cup are placed on the table, along with the seasonings: soy sauce, *wasabi* and thin slices of ginger.

Other fish and seafood

Many other intriguing fish dishes await adventurous diners. One of the most popular delicacies is eel, *unagi*. Dipped in a rich soy sauce and sake marinade and cooked over hot coals, it is delicious on a bed of rice *(una-don)*, or eaten from skewers *(kabayaki)*.

The type of fish dish you might find can depend on where you are in Japan. Crab and salmon cuisine is common in Hokkaido, while on Shikoku you can taste *katsuo no tataki* (charcoal-grilled bonito fish). A local favourite in Kagoshima is *sake zushi*, a casserole of rice, fish and vegetables in rice wine. On Western Honshu's southern coast the speciality is *fugu*, which comes from the highly poisonous blowfish and only to be eaten where the chef knows exactly what he's doing.

Throughout the country, fish might be served as *yakizakana* (broiled in salt) or *nizakana* (cooked in soy sauce). But for a taste of Japanese cuisine at its most refined, be sure to sample a *kaiseki ryori* meal. This involves several small and exquisitely presented dishes of fish with seaweed, vegetables, mushrooms and pickles.

The idea for *tempura*, tasty battered deep-fried seafood, was taken from the first Portuguese traders who came to Japan in the 16th century. These days you'll find everything from a slice of aubergine to an aromatic *shiso* leaf in your *tempura*. The dipping sauce for this dish combines soy sauce, horseradish and *sake*.

Meat

Though not traditionally meat-eaters, the Japanese have had a taste for beef, chicken and pork ever since the country opened up to the West in the 19th century.

Sukiyaki features thin slices of beef, chicken or pork cooked in a soy, sugar and *sake* mix at the table in an iron pan, together with onions, cabbage or spinach, mushrooms, tofu (bean curd) and vermicelli; you may dip each morsel in raw egg before eating. In *shabu-shabu*, the diners themselves boil very thin slices of beef and vegetables in a communal tabletop pan of steaming broth, then spice them with a variety of sauces. For *teppanyaki*, meat (or fish) and chopped vegetables are cooked on a flat open iron griddle, sometimes by the diners themselves.

The best beef for these dishes comes from Kobe. What makes Kobe beef so tender and tasty is the loving care the animals receive during the last six months of their life: the best rice and beans, with an occasional beer, and a daily massage to distribute the fat. Indeed, it's so deliciously tender that it is eaten raw in salads with dressings of ginger, soy, garlic and cayenne pepper.

Meat dishes are also available in restaurants serving foreign cuisine. Chinese food has had a great culinary tradition in Japan—specifically in Nagasaki—since the 17th century, and you will also find Korean, Thai and Indian restaurants. These days, American hamburger and fried chicken fast food chains can be found in all the big cities; Italian restaurants are generally excellent and the prices very reasonable.

Desserts
The Japanese do not make a big deal of desserts *(wagashi)*, which are mostly variations of Western-style cakes, *higashi* being dry cake, *namagashi* moist. *Rakugan* is a cake made from rice-flour. The Nagasaki speciality is *kasutera* (deriving from the Portuguese word *castella*), a sponge cake originally brought in by Portuguese sailors and perfected by Nagasaki chefs. Red beans *(azuki* and *anko)* are used in many puddings and jellies.

Drinks
For accompaniment, you'll want to try *sake*, Japanese rice wine. This is usually served hot in eggcup-sized tumblers—connoisseurs agree that only the best variety can be drunk cold. *Shochu* is a potent rice-brandy, and worth a try. Lager-type beer is extremely popular, and Japanese brews such as Asahi, Sapporo and Kirin are first-rate. Japanese-made whisky is usually reserved for consumption at whisky bars, and drunk with large amounts of water and ice.

If you don't want alcohol with your meal you can enjoy Japanese green tea *(o-cha)*, which is often brought to you free of charge in restaurants. You might be given brown tea *(bancha)* instead. Coffee *(kohii)* is popular, if expensive. The payoff is that you are free to sit at your café table for as long as you like.

A wide variety of drinks, both piping hot (indicated by a red band) and icy cold (blue band), are available in huge vending machines which you'll see wherever you go.

Ink sticks *(sumi)* are made from wood soot and glue, compressed to a thing of beauty.

SHOPPING

The high quality of the merchandise, the tasteful displays and the ultra-polite service make shopping in Japan a delight. A good way to begin is to explore a couple of the big department stores to acquaint yourself with the range of available goods and prices. All the main cities and towns are well supplied with department stores and brightly lit shopping arcades (at street level and below) selling everything from high-tech electrical equipment and haute couture to gourmet foods and the latest Japanese toys.

If you're interested in finding some of Japan's exquisite traditional products, search out the more rural parts of Honshu and less built-up regions of the country like Kyushu, Shikoku and Hokkaido. Flea markets are increasingly popular and a good way to hunt down a bargain. Always take along your passport for duty-free shopping—the 5% consumption tax will be refunded if you spend more than ¥10,000 on non-consumable items in one day at licensed tax-free shops, which includes most big department stores.

Where to shop
Of the main shopping areas in Tokyo, Ginza is the best known, but big stores are also found in Nihombashi, Shinjuku, Shibuya and other districts. Top-name fashion designers tend to congregate in Omote-Sando, Tokyo's Fifth Avenue, in trendy Shibuya. For cameras and videos try the stores near Shinjuku station. Akihabara, between the Imperial Palace and Ueno Park, is famous for electrical and electronic equipment. In Osaka, Den Den Town, just south of the downtown area, is also awash with electrical stores, while camera shops are located near Osaka Station.

Electrical equipment
Japan's supremacy in high-tech electrical equipment speaks for itself. On show in almost every electrical store will be the latest wizardry from world-famous names in photography and video,

and displays of cutting edge developments in calculators, radios, hi-fi equipment, computers and mini-computers. At the Sony Building in Tokyo's Ginza you'll get the chance to try out the latest gadgets before they've even reached the shops. Japan also specializes in watches, binoculars and clocks. But remember that prices may be higher in Japan than elsewhere in the Far East, such as Hong Kong. In electronics, battery-powered personal stereos are no problem, but check that the voltage and frequency of plug-in appliances are compatible with your home country supply.

Clothing

Japanese haute couture is stylish and well made, but bear in mind that Japanese clothes are often cut to fit smaller sizes than in Europe and America. Traditional clothing can make classic souvenirs. Silk is regarded as the queen of fabrics, and sumptuous silk kimonos look spectacular and may be hard to resist as special mementoes of your visit. The very best of them can reach up to ¥1 million. But whether you buy a silk tie, blouse, scarf, or pyjamas, the quality is likely to be impeccable.

Practical use is likely to be made of the light cotton—and far cheaper—variety of kimono, the *yukata*, which is the bathrobe provided in spas and ryokans. Even more comfortable is a *happi* coat, a type of jacket to wear for lounging around at home, and traditional wooden or straw-soled sandals.

Arts and handicrafts

The Japanese love of the delicate and the fragile can be seen in the minutely detailed scenes painted onto items such as eggshells, kites and bamboo-and-paper umbrellas, though they are not easy to transport. Consider also origami objects, intricately hand-folded from traditional Japanese paper (called *washi*)—or packets of the paper to fold your own. You will also see attractive ornaments made from materials such as lacquered leaves.

More robust lacquerware (*shikki*) always finds a use, from dinner tableware such as platters, bowls, and salad spoons to decorated boxes and even furniture, and it always demonstrates the concern for good design which permeates every aspect of Japanese life. You might also consider ceramic dinner sets painted with traditional scenes or modern abstractions, or beautifully decorated *sake* flasks and cups, coffee and tea cups, bowls and vases, often with the Satsuma black background with floral decorations.

A great memento of any visit to Western Honshu is an item of famous Bizen pottery. You can buy superb vases, tableware and ornaments, though this may well leave a large dent in your wallet. You can also buy superbly glazed and brilliantly colourful *nanzan* pottery from Zentsuji in Shikoku. Fine Kyushu porcelain is to be found in renowned pottery towns such as Imari and Arita.

Highly stylized woodblock prints are intrinsically Japanese, and you will still find Edo-era originals (by lesser known artists) at relatively affordable prices. Copies of famous Edo woodblock prints now appear on everything from coasters and placemats to mousepads and T-shirts.

Kyoto claims a 300-year-old doll-making tradition; the costumes are impeccably detailed. Look out for painted wooden dolls with wobbly heads, supposed to give warning of an earthquake.

Fierce or funny-looking, masks based on the *kabuki* and *noh* theatre make great gifts. Japan is also known for ornamental fans, made from silk or paper.

Cultured pearls grown in captive oysters are a Japanese speciality, and all grades are available, but genuine pearls are very expensive. Items made from mother of pearl, such as boxes and ashtrays, are sure to be popular back home.

A *yukata* makes an attractive and useful souvenir.

Flea markets

Flea markets, *nomi-no-ichi*, are generally held in the grounds of temples and shrines, so are atmospheric places to look out for antiques, furniture, tableware and bargain souvenirs. Famous markets to check out are at the Togo Shrine near Harajuku in Tokyo, held on the first, fourth and fifth Sunday of the month; the Kitano Temmangu Shrine in Kyoto on the 25th of each month; and the Toji temple market near Kyoto JR Station, held on the first Sunday and the 21st of each month.

All aspects of the life of a Sumo wrestler are strictly governed by traditional rules.

SPORTS

Japan is the home of famous sports such as judo, karate, aikido and kendo, so if you're interested in brushing up on your skills in the martial arts, this is the place to do it. The Japanese love the outdoor life as well, and with 80 per cent of the country being mountainous, activities such as hiking, mountaineering and skiing are highly popular. But nothing stirs the blood here like a sumo-wrestling tournament, and a visit to a sumo stadium during a major championship will provide an unrivalled insight into the passions and rituals that inform Japan's national sport.

In the mountains

Many excellent hiking trails are just a short distance from the big cities. Check out Nikko National Park, 100 km north of Tokyo, which has a varied terrain of marshland, lakes and extinct volcanoes; the Hira-san mountain range near Lake Biwa to the east of Kyoto or the stunning Japan Alps National Park, where you'll find breathtaking hiking trails in the valleys around Kamikochi. The Daisetsuzan National Park in Hokkaido is the largest in Japan, with several trails, magnificent mountain scenery and all manner of wildlife to be seen. In all of these areas, a day's hard hiking can be rounded off with a visit to an *onsen*, or hot spring.

Opportunities abound for mountain climbing around the country, but the most famous is Japan's emblematic Mt Fuji. At 3,776 m, this is the nation's highest mountain and extremely popular with climbers, especially in July and August, the "official" climbing season.

Skiing has long been a major sport in Japan. The main resorts are in Northern Honshu and Hokkaido, where the season runs from December to April. Many of the resorts now also cater to snowboarders.

By the sea

The warm waters and fine beaches of Okinawa provide excellent swimming almost the whole year round, but you can also enjoy a dip in the ocean on a day trip to Kamakura from Tokyo in the summer.

Surfers will want to head to the Inland Sea coast of Shikoku. International surf competitions are held around Toyo in Kochi prefecture, and you can surf at various points along the coast here. These beaches are also popular spots for snorkelling and scuba diving, though the main centre for the latter is Okinawa. The coral reefs around the island are spectacular and host to tropical fish and sea turtles.

Martial arts

Japanese martial arts are studied at training centres around the country. Judo is a sport based on using an opponent's strength to one's own advantage and is derived from the samurai discipline of jujutsu. Kendo also comes from the samurai. A form of fencing using lacquered bamboo sticks, it was originally a samurai training technique for sword fighting. Karate (literally "empty hands") originated in Okinawa in the 14th century at a time when peasants were banned from carrying weapons. Aikido is

Heavyweight entertainment. Sumo wrestlers, the *rikishi*, are divided into different ranks; the upper-rank, or *maku-uchi*, has five levels culminating in the *yokozuna*, or Grand Champions. Once they've attained this status, the *yokozuna* cannot be demoted, and if they can no longer cut the mustard are expected to retire. Wrestlers have a distinctive topknot called a *chon-mage*; but higher ranks can wear their hair in the *o-ichimage* style, named after the leaf of the ginko tree that it's said to resemble. The combatants enter the *dohyo*, the ring, with a great fanfare and go through an elaborate series of Shinto-inspired purifying movements known as the *shikiri*, while the kimono-attired *gyoji* (referees) look on. And so at last to the match itself. During a bout, the wrestlers wear nothing other than their *mawashi*, a 10-m-long piece of heavy silk folded into a loincloth and the key item used to manipulate opponents and achieve one of the 82 official winning techniques. These days, bouts have a time limit of four minutes and on a tournament day there will be anything up to 220 individual bouts, giving a full day of wrestling for fans to enjoy. That just leaves the question of how Sumo wrestlers get to be so big. The answer is simple: they eat large bowls of *chanko-nabe* every day, a special type of noodle dish made with fish or chicken that you can try for yourself at the Ryogoku Kokugikan Sumo stadium in Tokyo and many of the noodle shops in the nearby streets.

a more meditative sport that mixes unarmed combat techniques from karate with balletic movements from traditional Japanese dance, and calls on participants to concentrate their mental and physical energy in order to overcome opponents.

Spectator sports

Sumo was once practised during festivals at Shinto shrines; it's now a national obsession with blanket coverage on TV. Major tournaments are held throughout the year: in January, May and September at Tokyo's Ryogoku Kokugikan stadium; in March at Osaka's Furitsu Taiiku-kan gym; in July in Nagoya; and in November in Fukuoka in Kyushu.

Both professional and high school baseball are taken very seriously. The professional league has twelve teams, with the season running from April to October. For an unforgettable sporting night out, try to catch a game at the Tokyo Dome or the Koshien Stadium near Osaka.

After hosting the World Cup finals in 2002, Japan went soccer mad. The national league, known as the J-League, holds fixtures from March till November.

Surfing the waves near Kochi. | **Karate dojo.** | **A new ring, or *dohyo*, is made for each Sumo tournament.**

THE HARD FACTS

Airports

The main international gateways to Japan are Tokyo's Narita International Airport and the Kansai International Airport serving Osaka and Kyoto.

Narita Airport is around 65 km northeast of central Tokyo. Several different train services run to the city centre. JR Narita Express (N'EX) takes 60 minutes to Tokyo Station; seats must be reserved. JR Rapid Service takes 85 min to Tokyo Station; this is a normal commuter train without reservations and can get crowded. Keisei Skyliner serves Ueno Station (60 min), reservation advised. Keisei Limited Express is a normal commuter train serving Ueno Station (75 min). The Limousine bus service drops passengers at the main hotels in central districts like Akasaka, Shinjuku and Ikebukuro. It takes 60–90 minutes to reach the city centre.

Kansai International Airport opened in 1994 on a purpose-built island in Osaka Bay, 50 km south of the city. There are several means of transport to central Osaka and elsewhere. Nankai Rapit Limited Express serves Namba Station in central Osaka (35 min, reservation required). Nankai Airport Expess goes to Namba (45 min, normal commuter train, no reservations). JR Airport Express "Haruka" serves Tennoji Station (30 min) or Shin-Osaka Station (50 min) with both reserved and unreserved seats. The JR Kansai Airport Rapid Service, a regular commuter train, goes to Tennoji (50 min) or Osaka Station (70 min). The Limousine bus service stops at a number of downtown locations and hotels and takes 60 min to central Osaka, 100 min to Kyoto and 75 min to Kobe.

A high-speed ferry links Kansai and Kobe airports in 50 min (including shuttle bus) and also goes to Sumoto on Awaji Island (70 min).

All of the international airports have restaurants, cafés and shops, as well as foreign exchange, ATM and baggage storage facilities, mobile-phone hire, and visitor centres providing information and hotel booking services.

Climate

Japan has four distinct seasons, with cold winters, hot summers, and fine spring and autumn weather. Local climate variations are created throughout the year by the country's mountainous terrain, as well as the surrounding oceans and the influence of the nearby Asian landmass. Thus, for example, Hokkaido in the north, with an annual average temperature of 6°C, has long, severe winters with heavy snowfall, while the southern island of Kyushu, with an annual average temperature of 17°C, often basks in near tropical heat from spring till late autumn.

Overall, winter (which lasts approximately from December to early March) is influenced by the conjunction of cold, dry air from Siberia and warm, moist air from the Pacific. This leads to heavy snow and rainfall on the Sea of Japan side of the country and cold, drier weather on the Pacific side.

The summer months, from June to early September, are hot and humid, the result of dominant Pacific air masses; these also cause a rainy season to occur for a few weeks in early summer, usually in late May and June. Late summer is the typhoon season, when powerful storms lash the Pacific side of Japan in particular. The semi-tropical southern island of Okinawa sees typhoons anytime from June to October. The average daily temperature in Okinawa in July is 31°C and 20°C in December.

The best time to visit the country is in spring (from mid-March to early May) or autumn (from October to early December), when the climate is more stable, with mild temperatures and low rainfall. The cherry blossom season begins in Okinawa in February, reaches Kyushu in late February or early March and ends in Hokkaido in late April or early May; the autumnal leaves change colour starting in Hokkaido and continue in the opposite direction.

Communications

Japan's postal service is reliable, efficient and not especially expensive. Post offices can be recognised by a symbol showing a red letter T with a line across the top on a white background (post boxes are red with the same logo in white). They offer limited poste restante facilities, along with fax, international direct dialling and telegram services, and also sell stamps, aerogrammes and phonecards *(terefon kado)*. Note that letters can be addressed in Roman script.

International direct dialling is usually available from public phone boxes and will always be cheaper than using the hotel phone. Not all take cash: be sure to have a phonecard on you when out and about. International calls are 20% less in price if you dial between 7 p.m. and 11 p.m. or at weekends, and have a 40% reduction from 11 p.m. to 8 a.m.

Prepaid international phonecards can be bought from post offices, convenience stores, and vending machines. You can also hire a mobile phone and use your own SIM card.

For directory assistance call 104, for international directory enquiries call 0057. English-speaking international operators are on 0051. To telephone abroad from Japan, dial 00 1 + the country code (44 for UK) + area code (minus the initial zero) + local number. The country code for calling Japan from overseas is 81.

The Internet is extremely popular in Japan, with Internet cafés in all but the smallest towns, and online access offered free by many hotels and hostels.

Crime

Japan is one of the safest places for travellers anywhere in the world, though it's always wise to take precautions against theft, especially in the cities. Leave your valuables in the hotel safety deposit box where possible, beware of pickpockets in crowded places and always keep your money and passport well concealed, preferably in a money belt or sealable pocket. Make sure that cars are locked when unattended. Never leave bags or other objects that might look like they contain anything of value visible in a parked car.

Customs

Visitors over 20 years of age may import the following goods duty free: 400 cigarettes or 500 g of tobacco or 100 cigars or an assortment of these up to 500 g; three 750 ml bottles of any alcoholic beverages; 2 oz perfume; gifts to a value of ¥200,000. If you are unsure about any goods you are carrying be sure to notify a customs officer.

For more information visit: www.customs.go.jp/index_e.htm.

Driving

Road travel around Japan isn't as daunting as it might seem in prospect: most signposts are in Western lettering as well as Japanese characters, and other drivers generally keep to the rules. Going by car can also be the best way to reach some of the country's less accessible rural areas.

Driving is on the left. Petrol prices are no higher than European levels, though the tolls on expressways (motorways) are notoriously expensive at around ¥40 per kilometre. The speed limit on the expressway is a fairly low 80kph; in town it's 40kph, though given the volume of traffic, the limited amount of parking space and the excellent local transport system in Japanese cities, it's probably a good idea to avoid driving in them altogether.

Car hire is simple. You will need to be over 25 years of age (though this is lower with some firms) with a full driving licence and an International Driving Permit, obtainable from national automobile associations. Major international car hire firms such as Hertz and Avis are represented in Japan, alongside a plethora of local firms. Always check the rates of local companies as they might well be cheaper. Be aware that prices always go up during the main holiday seasons.

Electricity
The current is 100V, 50Hz. Plugs have two flat pins, as in the US. (US 110V equipment can be used, but anything rated 200 250V will need a transformer). European visitors will also need an adaptor for their electrical equipment.

Emergencies
In case of a serious emergency dial 119 for an ambulance or fire services, 110 for police.

Entry formalities
Tourists from EU states, the US, Australia, Canada and New Zealand will receive a 90-day visitor's visa on arrival in Japan. They should be in possession of a return or onward ticket and a passport valid for longer than the temporary visa (i.e. more than three months). If you are unsure about your status contact your nearest Japanese consulate or visit the Japan Ministry of Foreign Affairs website, www.mofa.go.jp. All foreigners entering Japan are fingerprinted and photographed.

Etiquette
Japanese courtesy is legendary. People always bow when they meet, and again on taking leave. You can shake hands if one is proffered. Business cards are exchanged at every opportunity—and studied carefully.

You should always take off your shoes before entering someone's house, or even a *ryokan*, a traditional Japanese inn, or *minshuku*, bed and breakfast accommodation. They must also be taken off before going inside a main temple building. Slippers are generally provided, especially in cold weather. Wear socks or stockings without holes!

It is not good form to eat while walking along the street or sitting on a subway train (this doesn't apply to Shinkansen or other inter-city trains); or to blow your nose too loudly, especially at the dinner table.

Health
No vaccinations are required for entry into Japan. The nation's medical facilities are of a high standard and there will usually be

an English-speaking medical practitioner available in the cities, though if you are in rural Japan the chances of finding one significantly diminish. Medical costs are high, so be sure to take out personal insurance for full emergency cover. If you require specialized prescription medicines remember to take enough with you to last for the duration of your stay.

Japan is generally a healthy place to be and the greatest hazard will probably be too much exposure to the sun. Visitors from cooler climates need to take great care to protect themselves against the sun's intensity during the summer months: always wear a high-factor sun block, sunhat and sunglasses when outside, and be especially careful between 11 a.m. and 3 p.m., when the sun is at its most powerful. Be sure to carry a bottle of water if you're out for a long walk.

Holidays

Public holidays are as follows:

January 1	*Gantan* (New Year's Day)
2nd Mon Jan	*Seijin-no-hi* (Coming-of-Age Day)
February 11	*Kenkokukinen-no-hi* (National Foundation Day)
March 20 or 21	*Shunbun-no-hi* (Spring Equinox)
April 29	*Showa-no-hi* (Start of Golden Week)
May 3	*Kempo kinen-bi* (Constitution Day)
May 4	*Midori-no-hi* (Greenery Day)
May 5	*Kodomo-no-hi* (Children's Day)
3rd Mon July	*Umi-no-hi* (Marine Day)
3rd Mon Sept	*Keiro-no-hi* (Respect for the Elderly Day)
September 23 or 24	*Shunbun-no-hi* (Autumn Equinox)
2nd Mon Oct	*Taiku-no-hi* (Health Sports Day)
November 3	*Bunka-no-hi* (Culture Day)
November 23	*Kinro kansha-no-hi* (Labour Thanksgiving Day)
December 23	*Tenno Tanjobi* (Emperor's Birthday)

During Golden Week and over the New Year holiday, transport and hotels are likely to be extremely busy. If you plan to travel during these periods be sure to book well in advance.

Language

The national and official language is Japanese, the standard form of which is called *hyojungo* and spoken throughout the country. There are also several regional dialects with their own vocabulary and phrases. Although

English is taught to all Japanese schoolchildren it isn't widely understood, especially amongst the older population; should you need directions, for example, ask a younger adult and if necessary show them the name of the hotel, shop or district in writing, as this gets over the tricky problem of pronunciation. Staff at large hotels and tourist offices in big cities will speak some English.

Written Japanese is comprised of three different scripts—*kanji*, the Chinese pictograms which run into thousands and are fiendishly difficult to remember; *hiragana*, a supplementary system developed to fill in the inevitable gaps that *kanji* faced in expressing the many differences between Chinese and Japanese; and *katakana*, a more recent script used to express foreign loan words like *biiru* (beer) and *hoteru* (hotel). Spoken Japanese is an easier proposition, as the language is regular, with few inflexions and fairly straightforward tenses. Japanese people always appreciate any attempt made by foreigners to speak their language. Here are some of the key phrases that will be useful to know—and are sure to draw praise from the locals:

Good morning	*o-hayo gozaimas*
Good afternoon	*konnichi-wa*
Good evening	*konbanwa*
Goodbye	*sayonara*
Excuse me	*sumimasen*
Do you speak English?	*eigo ga hanasemas(u) ka?*
Where is…?	*…wa doko des(u) ka?*
How much is…?	*…ikura des(u) ka?*
Thanks	*domo*
Thank you	*domo arigato*
Cheers!	*Kampai!*
This is delicious	*oishi des*

Media

There are three daily newspapers in English, the *Asahi Shimbun*, the *Japan Times* and the *Daily Yomiuri*. You can buy them at stations, bookstores and newsagents in the downtown areas of larger cities. Foreign newspapers are rare commodities in Japan, though you will find major international magazines on sale in big city bookshops.

A number of radio channels cater for Japan's foreign population, such as InterFM (76.1) in Tokyo and FM Cocolo (76.5) in Kansai. News buffs should also be sure to take a shortwave radio and a list of local wavelengths from the BBC World Service.

Larger international hotel chains will provide satellite channels on TV, which will carry English-language news stations such as CNN and BBC World. If your TV has the right system built into it you can also listen to a simultaneous English translation of the Japanese NHK news at night at 7 p.m. and 10 p.m.

Money

The unit of currency is the yen (abbreviated to ¥). Coins are issued in denominations of ¥1, ¥5, ¥10, ¥50, ¥100 and ¥500; banknotes have values of ¥1000, ¥2000, ¥5000 and ¥10,000.

International credit cards and travellers cheques are accepted at large hotels and upscale restaurants and shops in cities and popular tourist areas, and increasingly in more out-of-the-way places.

You can withdraw cash from ATMs at banks with a debit card using your own PIN code. The ATMs at major international banks such as Citibank in Tokyo, Osaka and Kyoto accept foreign cards, as do all post office machines.

Opening hours

The following times are a general guide, and some of them may be subject to local variations.

Banks are open Monday to Friday 9.30 a.m.–3 p.m., and on Saturdays until noon, except for the second Saturday of the month when they are always closed.

Main post offices usually open Monday to Friday 9 a.m.–7 p.m. and 9 a.m.–3 p.m. on Saturday.

Shops are usually open daily 9 a.m.–5 p.m., though some close on Sunday. Department stores tend to open 10 a.m.–7 or 8 p.m.

Public transport

Air. The excellent network of internal flights operated by JAL and ANA airlines will be of particular use for those travellers who only have limited time in Japan but want to get to the furthest corners of the country, in particular Okinawa, Kyushu and Hokkaido. Prices are surprisingly low—not much different from Shinkansen train fares; overseas residents can take advantage of advance-purchase reductions and such things as JAL's Welcome to Japan or ANA's Visit Japan Fare.

Intercity Buses. There is an extensive long-distance bus system throughout the country. It is considerably less expensive than taking an express train, for example, but naturally, it's also much slower, and unless you have plenty of time is probably only a sensible option for travel to more out of the way places not served by the train network.

Trains. The pride and glory of Japan's public transport system is its railways: fast, reliable and, in the shape of the high-speed Shinkansen bullet trains, the very image of the nation's post-war technological success. The network comes under the umbrella of the Japan Railways Group (JR), which is composed of a number of privatized rail companies. The system is completely integrated, however, in terms of timetables and ticketing.

There are several different types of train. Local *(futsu)* stop at every station. Express *(kyuku)* miss out some stations. Rather confusingly, Limited Express *(tokkyu)* are faster than express trains. Shinkansen super-express are also known as bullet trains. The Shinkansen are the sleek thoroughbreds of the network and race across the country from Hakata in Kyushu to Hachinohe in northern Honshu at speeds of up to 300 kph. The latest Nozomi Shinkansen cover the 552.6 km between Tokyo and Osaka in around 2 hr 20 min. Some trains require reservations, but this can be done up to 15 minutes before departure times, and the service is free. It is advisable to book your seats if you are travelling with several bags or suitcases.

Ordinary Class carriages are always clean and comfortable and, on the Shinkansen and many Limited Express trains, served by a regular trolley service with drinks and snacks. Shops selling *bento* (a lunch box) are on every Shinkansen railway platform. First-class carriages are called Green Cars, identified by a green flower design on the door.

Shinkansen tickets are expensive, so if you're planning on travelling around Japan to any extent be sure to purchase a JR Rail Pass. This must be bought before you leave your home country—you cannot buy it in Japan. You should purchase an Exchange Order at a JR agent where you live and then obtain your pass at a mainline station in Japan. The pass gives unlimited travel on all JR trains other than the Nozomi Shinkansen, including metropolitan JR services in Osaka and Tokyo, for 7, 14, or 21 days. Regional passes such as the JR Hokkaido, JR Kyushu, JR West and JR East, are also available.

To find out where your nearest JR agent is, or to check current prices and conditions for rail passes, visit www.japanrailpass.net. For general information on JR trains, visit www.japanrail.com.

Ferries. Numerous ferry services link up Japan's islands. The Honshu-Hokkaido crossing takes around 20 hours, while the Osaka-Kyushu route, arriving at Beppu in the morning, is 13 hours. Boats bound for Okinawa from Tokyo are like mini-cruises, taking up to 45 hours; from Kobe it's around 30 hours and from Kagoshima in Kyushu it's 21 hours. You can book a cabin on these boats; the cheapest way is to sleep on a *tatami* mat in one of the large, general rooms.

Taxis
Taxis are readily available, but expensive. It's wise to have your destination written in Japanese—as well as the language problem, Japanese cities have the world's most complex system of addresses. Note that the passenger doors open and close by remote control.

Time
Japan is on GMT+9, all year round. When it's noon in Tokyo, it will be 3 a.m. in London in winter (4 a.m. in summer), and 10 p.m. the previous evening in New York in winter, 11 p.m. in summer.

Tipping
Tipping is not a Japanese custom, and there is no obligation to leave a tip for waiters, room maids, taxi drivers or hotel porters; in fact they will probably be refused. However, a service charge is added to bills at hotels, nightclubs and better restaurants, while porters at airports, ports and rail stations charge a set fee for carrying luggage.

Toilets
There is no difficulty finding public toilets in Japan: they are available at virtually every temple and park, and can always be found in shopping areas in towns and cities. They are often of the "squat" rather than sit-down variety. If this is a problem, make sure you take advantage of the facilities in cafés, restaurants, tourist hotels and museums, which tend to have Western style toilets available. Some are very high tech, with heated seats, automatically lifting lids, music, water jets and other gadgets. There's no need to panic on long train journeys: modern express trains have both types.

Public toilets do not always have toilet paper and rarely provide towels or hot-air machines for hand drying: be sure to have tissues with you when you go out (packets of tissues are frequently handed out free at railway stations as advertising—it's always worth taking them).

Tourist information
For more information before you leave home, check for your nearest Japan National Tourist Organisation: www.jnto.go.jp.

The main Tourist Information Centre in Tokyo is on the 10th floor of the Kotsu Kaikan Building, 2-10-1 Yuraku-cho Chiyoda-ku (in front of JR Yurakucho Station), where there will be English-speaking members of staff and publications in English.

Water
Tap water is generally safe to drink throughout Japan but most people prefer mineral water.

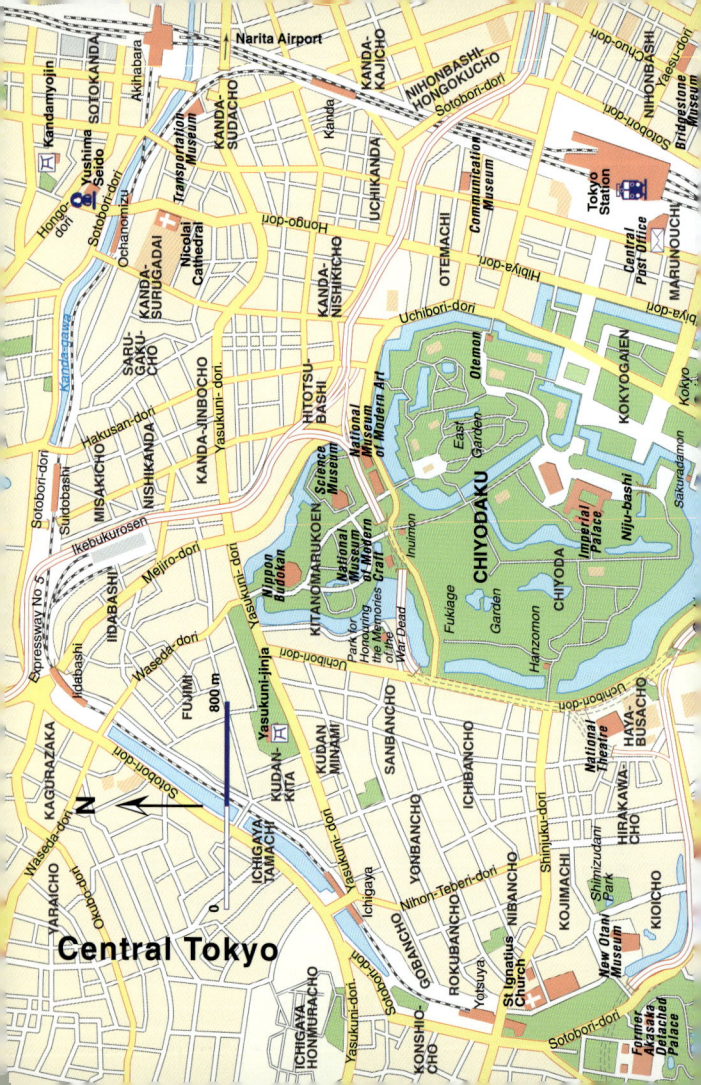

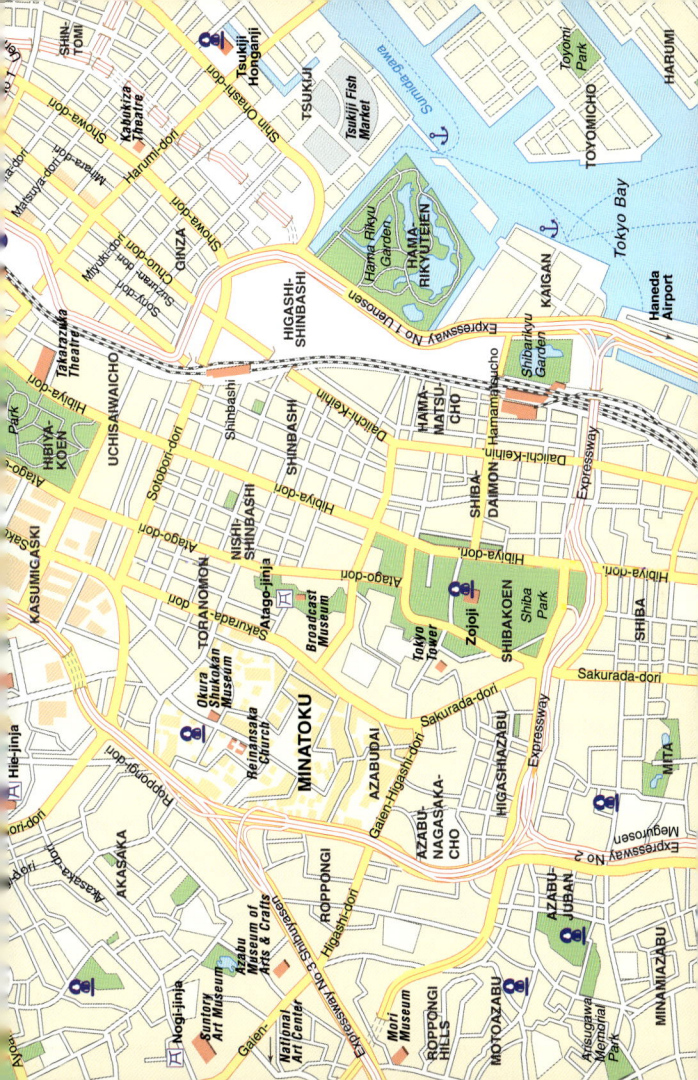

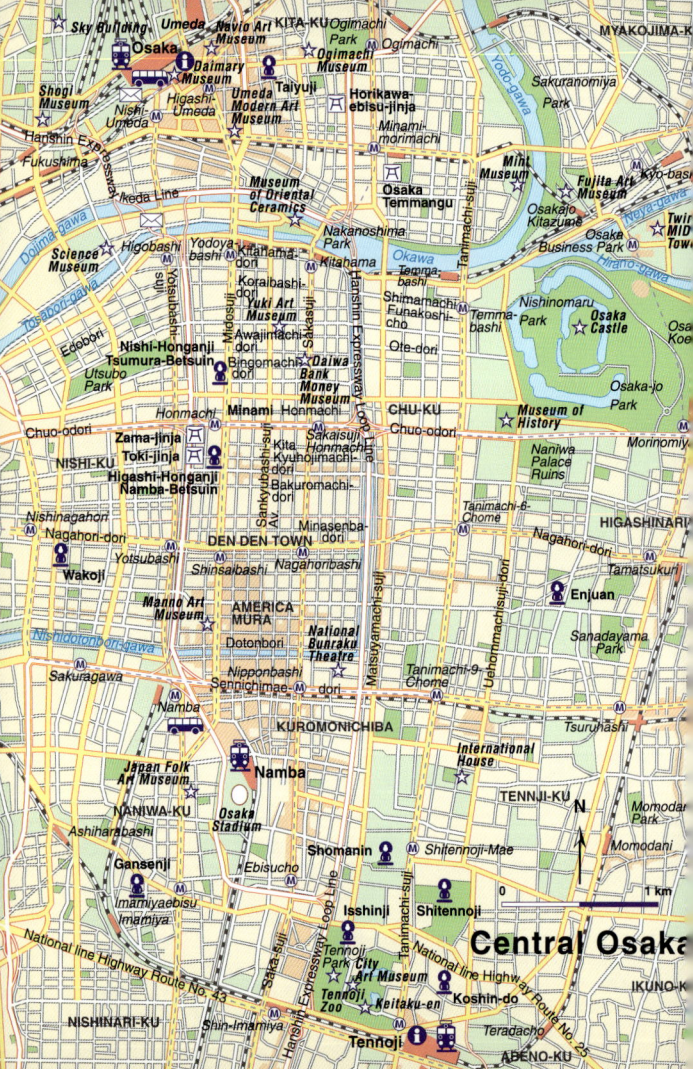

INDEX

Ainu 82
Airports 100
Akan National Park 64–66
Ashi, Lake 32
Awaji-shima 58
Bathing etiquette 65
Beppu 73
Bizen 53
Chusonji 33
Climate 100–101
Communications 101–102
Crime 102
Customs 102
Daibutsu 29
Dogo Spa 69
Driving 102–103
Electricity 103
Emergencies 103
Entry Formalities 103
Etiquette 103
Erimo, Cape 64
Fuji, Mount 31–32
Fuji-Go-ko 31–32
Geisha 40
Goryo-kaku 61–62
Hakodate 61–62
Hakone 32
Health 103–104
Himeji 47, 50–51
Hiroshima 55–57
   A-Bomb Dome 55
   Peace Memorial Hall 57
   Peace Memorial Museum 57
   Peace Memorial Park 55
Holidays 104
Horyuji 44–45
Ibusuki 79
Ikuchi-jima 59
Inland Sea 58–59
Jozankei Onsen 63
Kagoshima 77–79
   Foreigners' Residence 78
   Iso Gardens 78
   Monuments 79
   Shiroyama Park 78
Kakunodate 33
Kamakura 28–29
Kobe 49–50
   Kitano 50

Kobe City Museum 50
Kobe Maritime Museum 50
   Port area 49–50
   Port Island 50
Kochi 70–71
Kotohiragu 70
Kuju 74
Kurashiki 54
Kurosawa, Akira 82–83
Kushiro Shitsugen National Park 64
Kyoto 35–43
   Arashiyama 43
   City Centre 35–37
   East Kyoto 37–41
   Fushimi-Inari Taisha 43
   Ginkakuji 41
   Heian Shrine 41
   Imperial Palace 35–37
   Kinkakuji 41
   Kyomizu-dera 39
   Kyoto National Museum 39
   Municipal Museum of Modern Art 39
   National Museum of Modern Art 39
   Nijo Castle 37
   Ninomaru Palace Garden 37
   Nishiki Market 37
   Path of Philosophy 41
   Ponto-cho 37
   Ryoanji 5, 43
   Sanjusangendo 39
   South Kyoto 43
   Tenryuji 43
   West Kyoto 41–43
Language 104–105
Literature 83–84
Manga 84
Matsushima 32–33
Matsuyama 47, 69
Media 105–106
Miyajima 57–58
Money 106
Mt Aso National Park 74
Nagasaki 74–77
   Atomic Bomb Museum 77

   Central Station 75
   Dejima 75–76
   Glover Gardens 76–77
   Hypocentre Park 77
   Inasa, Mt 75
   Kofukuji 75
   Madame Butterfly 77
   Meganebashi 75
   Peace Park 77
   Shofukuji 75
   Sofukuji 75
   Urakami 77
Naha 81
Nao-shima 58–59
Nara 43–44
   Kasuga Taisha 44
   Kofukuji 43–44
   Nara National Museum 44
   Nigatsudo 44
   Todaiji 28, 44
Naruto 70
Nikko 29–30
Noboribetsu 63
Okayama City 53
Omi-shima 59
Opening hours 106
Osaka 45–49
   City Art Museum 49
   Fujita Art Museum 46–47
   Minami district 47–49
   Mint Museum 46
   Museum of Oriental Ceramics 46
   Osaka Aquarium 49
   Osaka Castle 47
   Osaka Museum of History 47
   Shitennoji 49
   Umeda Sky Building 46
   Universal Studios Japan 49
Pilgrimage 71
Rishiri-Rebun-Sarobetsu National Park 67
Sakurajma 79
Sapporo 62–63
Seikan Tunnel 62
Shikotsu-Toya National Park 63

120 INDEX

Shinto 84
Shiretoko National Park 66
Shodo-shima 58
Shuri 81
Sumo 98
Takamatsu 70
Taxis 108
Tea ceremony 11
Time 108
Tipping 108
Theatre 20
Toilets 108
Tokyo 17–26
  Akasaka district 18
  Asakusa 21–22
  Asakusa Kannon Temple 21
  City Centre 18–21
  Edo Castle 18
  Edo-Tokyo Museum 22
  Ginza 20
  Harajuku 25
  Imperial Palace 18
  Kabuki-cho 25–26
  Kabukiza Theatre 20
  Kappabashi-dori 21–22
  Kitanomaru Park 20–21
  Meiji Shrine 25
  Mori Art Museum 23–25
  Mori Tower 19
  National Art Center 19
  National Museum of Modern Art 20–21
  National Museum of Western Art 22
  National Science Museum 22
  Nippon Budokan 21
  Omote-sando-dori 25
  Ota Museum 25
  Otemon 18
  Roppongi 19
  Ryogoku 22
  Science Museum 20
  Sensoji 21
  Shibuya 23–25
  Shinjuku 23–26
  Shitamachi Museum 22
  Sumida River 22–23
  Sumo Museum 22
  Tokyo Metropolitan Government Office 26
  Tokyo National Museum 22
  Tokyo Tower 19
  Treasure Museum 25
  Tsukiji market 23
  Ueno Park 22
  Yasukuni Shrine 21
  Zozoji 19
Tourist information 108
Towada-Hachimantai National Park 33
Transport 106–107
Ukiyo-e 85
Wakkanai 66–67
Water 108
World War II Battlefields 81
Yashima 70
Yokohama 26–27
  Bund 26
  Chinatown 27
  Cosmo World 26
  Landmark Tower 26
  Marine Tower 27
  Maritime Museum 26
  Mitsubishi Minato Mirai Industrial Museum 26
  Sankei-en 27
  Silk Centre and Museum 27
  Sky Garden 26
  Yamashita Park 26–27
Yufuin 73
Zen garden 5
Zentsuji 69

General editor
Barbara Ender-Jones

Design
Karin Palazzolo

Layout
Luc Malherbe
Matias Jolliet

Photo credits
Agnès Curchod: p. 1
Corbis/Kaehler: p. 2 (cranes)
Derwal/hemis.fr: p. 2 (Harajuku fashions)
istockphotos.com/tkorocky: p. 2 (lucky cat)
Claude Hervé-Bazin: p. 2 (fountain)

Maps
JPM Publications,
Mathieu Germay

Copyright © 2008
JPM Publications S.A.
12, avenue William-Fraisse,
1006 Lausanne, Suisse
information@jpmguides.com
http://www.jpmguides.com/

All rights reserved. No part of this book may be reproduced or transmitted in any form or by any means, electronic or mechanical, including photocopying, recording or by any information storage and retrieval system without permission in writing from the publisher.

Every care has been taken to verify the information in the guide, but the publisher cannot accept responsibility for any errors that may have occurred. If you spot an inaccuracy or a serious omission, please let us know.

Printed in Switzerland
11766.00.1992
Weber/Bienne
Edition 2008

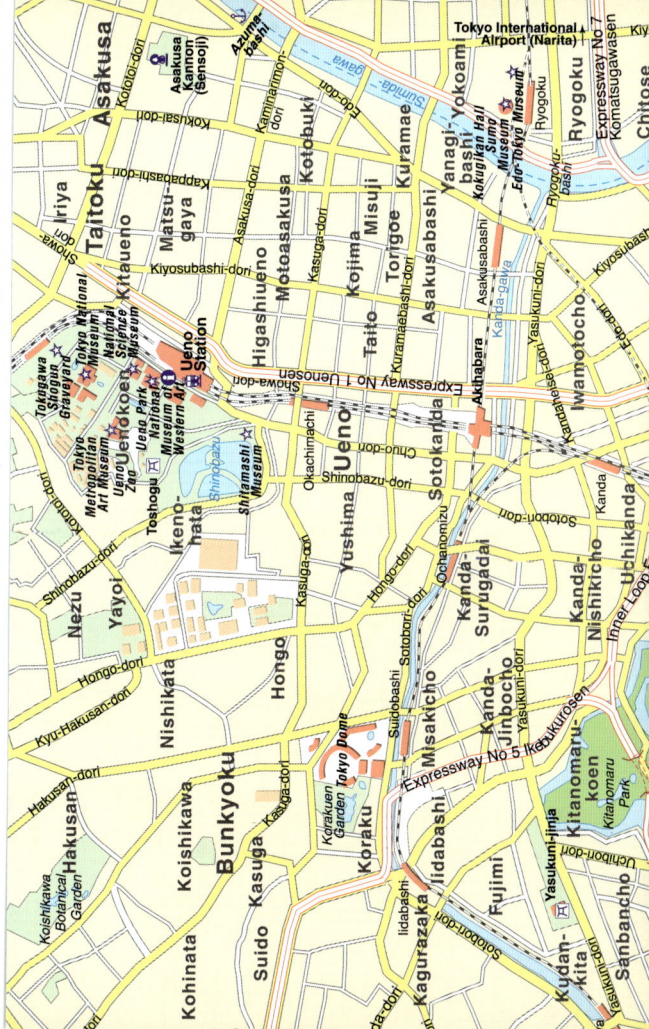

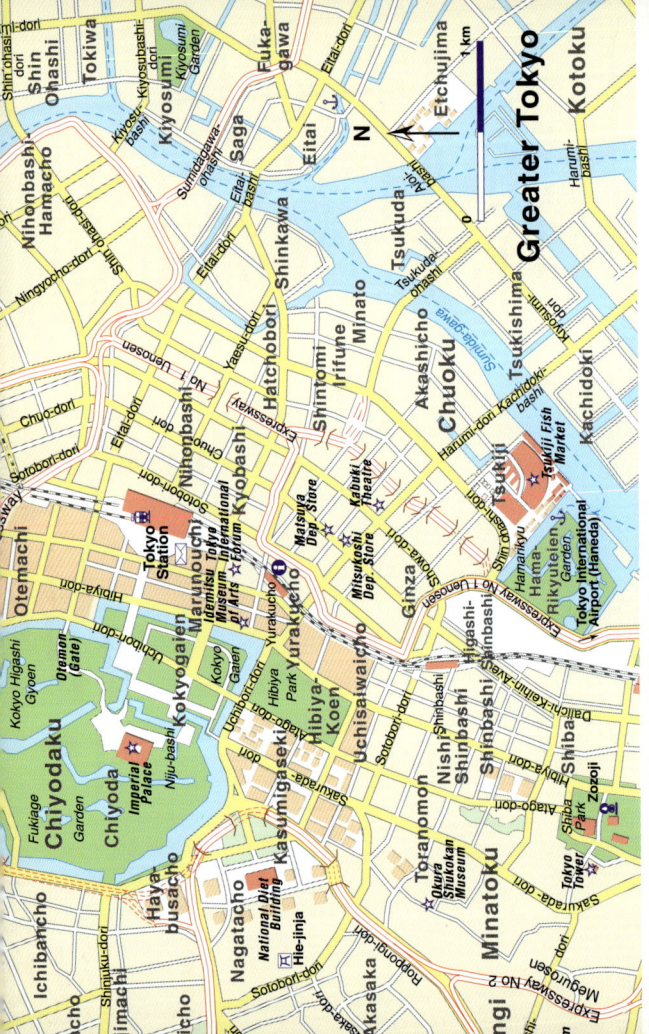